S0-CBH-266

TRAINING
FOR
NORdic SkiiNq

edited by Dave Prokop

Published by
World Publications

CAMROSE LUTHERAN COLLEGE
Library

Copyright © 1974 by NORDIC WORLD MAGAZINE

First Printing - January 1975
Second Printing - December 1976

$T\partial C$

All rights reserved. No information in
this book may be reprinted in any form with-
out permission from the publisher.

Library of Congress Catalog Card Number: 74-16795
ISBN: 0-89037-052-4

WORLD PUBLICATIONS, Box 366, Mountain View, CA 94040

GV
854.9
C7
T 72 | 24,634

CONTENTS

Cover Photo: Canada's Matti Maki in the '74 North American championships.
(Jarl Omholt-Jensen)

FOREWORD

The complexity of training for cross-country ski racing is probably unequaled among endurance sports. In terms of pure physical conditioning, for instance, cross-country ski racing at an advanced level requires not only tremendous cardiovascular endurance (since the cross-country skier burns more oxygen when he's racing than any other endurance athlete) but great overall body strength as well (for the total body effort of poling and striding). Cross-country skiing is also an extremely technical (or technique-oriented) sport, much more so than long distance running, for instance. The skier, therefore, must also devote considerable attention to this aspect of training. As in all endurance sports, that great unmeasurable but vital quality—mental strength—must also be properly developed if the skier is to be successful in top competition.

As if the above training requirements were not enough, the cross-country skier must contend with having no snow to train on for a large part of the year. As veteran US nordic racer Bob Gray says in the opening article of this book: "Runners run, swimmers swim, tennis players play tennis, etc. What does the cross-country skier do? Well, for most of the year he does everything but ski."

The latter situation, while forcing the skier to incorporate more variety into his program (which makes the training more interesting and enjoyable), also confronts him with the question of how to make his off-season or dry-land training the most effective for his sport. Is a combination of running, for cardiovascular endurance, and weight lifting, for strength, the best approach? Or should one rely on activities that are more closely related to cross-country skiing—roller skiing, for instance, and simulation exercises such as hill bounding with poles? Perhaps it would be better to do a mixture of ski-related and non-ski-related activities? Does it make any difference what you do? Maybe it's best to simply forget about cross-country skiing altogether during the spring and summer, and instead train and compete as a runner, cyclist, kayaker, etc.—as some skiers do.

Compared to cross-country ski training, the training for sports like distance running and swimming seems simple and straight-forward. Despite this, it's safe to say that the number of training books published in North American on running and swimming outnumber training books published on cross-country skiing by about 10 to 0—the 0 explained by the fact that heretofore there has been no book published in North America specifically on training for cross-country ski racing. This book is our attempt to make up at least partially for the literature deficiency in this area.

Some of the world's most knowledgeable people on nordic skiing and training have contributed to this book. The list includes veteran American racers such as Bob Gray, Larry Damon and Peter Davis, national coaches Bjorger Pettersen (Canada) and Marty Hall (United States), internationally-known Scandinavian coaches David Johansson (Sweden) and Rolf Kjaernsli (Norway), *Nordic World* magazine senior European contributor Lennart Strand (Sweden) and respected American nordic authorities John Caldwell and Sven Wiik. The contributions of these men and others has resulted in a book which covers a wide variety of training topics—general training philosophies, roller skiing and off-season training, setting up a year-round program, descriptions of national programs, training for junior and collegiate competitors, senior (over 40) skiers and citizen racers, weight training, etc. The last chapter in the book is devoted to the training schedules of some of the best nordic racers in North America and Europe. Included in this chapter is an inspiring profile on Sweden's legendary Sixten Jernberg, winner of more Olympic and world championship nordic medals than any other skier in history.

The book, of course, does not include all possible approaches to training. Nor are the ideas in the book necessarily to be regarded as "chiselled-in-stone" truths. Rather, the articles on these pages reflect the individual opinions, ideas and approaches to training of the respective authors. Indeed, as you read the book you can't help but notice some interesting differences of opinion or approach. Some examples:

● Bob Gray says in his article, "While training must be an important part of your life, take care that it doesn't become the *only* part." And John Caldwell says essentially the same: "There's more to life than just concentrating on one single purpose, no matter what that purpose is." But Sweden's dedicated world champion racer Thomas Magnusson states boldly, when asked how he relaxes, "I almost never relax. No time for it. I train, work, eat and rest, and train again."

● Four-time US Olympian Larry Damon stresses the importance of organization in training and having "things written down, both records of what you did in training and what you intend to do." But Martha Rockwell, the most successful nordic racer, internationally, that the US has yet produced, says, "I keep no records, no charts, no 'training log,' etc., nor do I adhere to a written 'program.' "

● Canadian national coach Bjorger Pettersen says, "In the early '70's Canada went through stages of experimental weight training. Along with most other nations, we have found weight training to be unsuccessful (for cross-country skiing)." US head coach Marty Hall, on the other hand, is staunchly in favor of weight training for his team.

Confusing? Perhaps. But one of the most fascinating things about training is the variety of approaches and views possible. And isn't the objective consideration of these approaches and views, coupled with one's own experiences and ideas, the intelligent way to develop one's personal training philosophy and approach?

We wish to thank all those who contributed articles and information to this book. Many of the coaches and athletes had to free time in a very busy fall schedule to assist with this effort. Canada's Bjorger Pettersen, for example, wrote the first two-thirds of his article at a hectic time when he had 30 members of his team to look after at a fall training camp in British Columbia. He sent us the final part of his article from Sweden, where he and his skiers had gone at the conclusion of their Canadian camp. A letter coach Pettersen sent with the concluding section of his article was return-addressed: "Somewhere between Canada and Sweden."

Several people whose names will not appear anywhere else in this book deserve special thanks for their help with translation—Professor John Weinstock of the University of Texas, Pentti Kanerva of Palo Alto, California, and Jan Herhold of our own office. Jan not only helped with translation but also did the layout on the book.

1

Approach To Training

by Bob Gray

Thirty-five-year-old Bob Gray of Putney, Vt. has been an international nordic racer for 12 years and a serious nordic skier almost twice that long. Best at the longer distances, Bob was the US 50-kilometer champion in '71 and '72, 27th place finisher in the world famous and demanding Vasaloppet (86.5 kilometers) in '70, and the first American in the 50-kilometer at the '74 world championships. A two-time Olympian ('68 and '72), Bob was the number one ranked US nordic skier in the '72-'73 season.

It's November 13, 1974, as I write this in Putney, Vermont. Looking out at the hills that surround me, it occurs to me just how much the change of seasons has to do with one's approach to training.

Today is one of those cold, grey November days with just enough of a chill wind to make you feel the urgency of something coming. That something is winter and it's just around the corner. It feels natural to just be out somewhere running, rushing, exerting, preparing for the season ahead, getting ready for winter and skiing.

I have been training for cross-country skiing for more than 20 years and this training has always corresponded with the passage of the seasons from summer into winter. Increased physical activity at this time of year has always seemed like the natural thing to do. Therefore, it is difficult for me to isolate training as just a means to an end. And, perhaps understandably, I feel that in training a more natural approach is the key to success.

As I discuss training you must remember that my experiences have been mostly limited to cross-country skiing. Athletes from other backgrounds might well have different thoughts.

Cross-country skiing is quite a different and special sport. It is much more subtle that it first appears and needs to be treated accordingly. It takes years to develop the fine points cross-country skiing demands both in training and racing.

In most other sports you are able to train for your sport by doing your sport. Runners run, swimmers swim, tennis players play tennis, etc. What does a cross-country skier do? Well, for most of the year he does everything but ski.

He runs, hikes, bikes and paddles, all the time trying to remember that he is actually a skier. The recent invention of roller skis for summer training has helped but in my opinion these devices still leave a lot to be desired.

It is easy then for a cross-country skier to become confused during his training and even to be led astray from time to time. Sometimes skiers become runners for awhile, or kayakers, or hikers or even cyclists. Still, as long as they "return to their senses" in time to prepare for skiing, nothing is lost. In fact, they may even have gained from the diversion.

I believe it is the mental approach to skiing and ski training that makes the difference in the end. It's not so much what you do in training as how you go about doing it from a psychological point of view. Don't get me wrong, however; you have to train for cross-country skiing and you have to train hard and year-round. Still it has never been enough to just put in the miles, the hours, and expect the results to follow automatically. There is more to it than the physical, much more. You have to look at what you are doing, think about what you are doing and learn to put it all together.

Training for cross-country skiing should become a part of your life, not something extra, a choice that must be made each day. Training can't be a sacrifice because a cross-country skier's career is such a long-term proposition. To become a successful cross-country competitor takes years. You have to love the sport. If your training becomes too much of a sacrifice, your love will cool and so will your skiing. That's why I feel so strongly about a training program that is natural, enjoyable and interesting. As a cross-country skier you are going to spend at least 10 years of your life training. Don't sacrifice those years; make them a valuable part of your life.

While training must be an important part of your life, take care that it doesn't become the *only* part. There is a danger in becoming obsessed with your training so that you forget why you are training, only that you must train. Enjoy your training. Don't forget where you are going and just how you plan to get there. Too often I have seen skiers who were unbeatable in August but pushovers in January.

The mental and physical progression is the most important part of your training. Don't wear your mind out in summer and fall training, and leave nothing for the winter. The most important part of the year is the racing season. Isn't that what you are training for? This is when your energy and concentration should be at their peak. And December is not the end of it all either. It's just the beginning. It is the next *four* months that count.

In my experience the transition from dry-land to snow is always hard. There is a letdown. Now, more than ever, you have to think about what you are doing so that you can continue to build your progression through the winter to a peak in March. And in-between, so to speak, is winter, the most difficult part of the whole season. You know it will be difficult to hang on until the very end, until March, without losing it all. Still, that is what you have to do. Otherwise, the rest of the year, the other eight months of training will have been wasted. Are you going to be a cross-country skier or one who just trains for skiing?

To repeat once again, what I am talking here is not what you do in training as much as how you go about doing it. Don't get caught up by just "putting in time." Training shouldn't be a job. Training should be enjoyable. Oh, there are moments when training is anything but enjoyable. But generally training should be a pleasure.

Another danger in training is confusing training and racing. It is all too easy for a training workout to end up in a race—especially when training with your peers. I feel that an individual has only so many great races in him (or her, excuse me, Martha Rockwell) and it is possible to waste many of these great races in training. Train hard, train well, but save those great days for the races.

The whole key to training effectively is getting to know yourself physically and mentally. To begin with, you have to be absolutely honest with yourself. Are you really tired, or just lazy? Do you need a rest or a fierce workout? You have to learn to control your workouts with honest hard days and honest easy days, depending on your needs. Basically, cross-country is a lonely sport, which is all the more reason why you have to know yourself. A coach can help, but he can't always know what is really the truth, what you're feeling. Only you can do that and this you must learn to do.

On most days, I think you should finish "on top of" the workout. In other words, you should have a little left over, wanting to go again, ready for tomorrow. Still, there are some days when maybe you really need to "put yourself under" and hurt, just so you don't forget what a hard effort feels like. However, you can only take so much pain before you begin to hold back a little and holding back can get to be a habit. Save most of the real hurting for the races, therefore. Somehow, it doesn't hurt so much in a race and it all seems worthwhile at the end.

Anyway, racing is what is all boils down to—all those days, months, years of training, planning, dreaming. How do you successfully concentrate all that into a single race? Those who can do it are the winners. The rest of us, well, what do we do? Train harder? Train more? Maybe we should look more carefully at what we are doing and how we do it. Learn to concentrate, to put it all together when it counts. That's what the winners do.

THE INDIVIDUAL APPROACH
by Larry Damon

Like his fellow Vermonter Bob Gray, Larry Damon is a veteran international nordic skier, having been a member of *four* US Winter Olympic teams ('56, '64, '68 and '72). An engineer by profession, he is now the head nordic instructor at the Trapp Family Lodge in Stowe, Vermont, North America's largest and best known nordic skiing center.

Training for cross-country skiing is a very broad subject which has no steadfast rules. Individuals are so vastly different physically and psychologically that when a coach sets up a hard-and-fast training program for a team, 10 times out of 10, half of the team members are dissatisfied and their performance curves start down.

In this article I wish to stress the individual approach to training. I feel the average coach fails to recognize the importance of the individual approach and consequently fails by at least 25 percent to get the best out of his team. The failure comes in the coach not spending enough time with each individual and guiding each individual to the best approach—for him—to attack the workload the coach thinks the team needs. With some team members, the coach should even consider the possibility that the workload might be too much.

The popular approach in coaching, of course, and seemingly the easiest one, is for the coach to *order* the team to do the training. This method not only fails to produce the best possible individual and team performances, but the coach invariably finds himself facing the typical team problems such as dissension, strain-type injuries, sickness and low morale.

THE COACH'S JOB

As I see it, the real job of the coach is to *teach* and *show* athletes how to do things. He should also keep some sort of individual improvement records or curves. As a mental or morale aid, he should not only encourage the team but each individual separately.

In the newer approaches to education, teachers are spending more time with individual students in the hope of better serving their more intelligent, but perhaps also more sensitive students. Teachers are also seeking more student participation in both the subject matter at hand and also within the teaching structure.

I think coaching should be more like this. The coach should be more open to the desires of the team members and each athlete should be encouraged to follow his own pattern and even his own system of training. The higher the level of team quality and experience, the more these coaching methods should be practiced. The coach is only a guide-post, or a handy expert, and he should *love* being only that.

By way of personal background data, I have competed on four US Olympic nordic teams in cross-country skiing. I lived and skied in Norway for five years. I have raced on foot at all distances from the half mile to the marathon, with a 10th place in the 1962 Boston marathon as the high point of my running career. I am still competing at age 41 and can at present average five minutes per mile over five miles as a foot runner. As a cross-country skier, I am limited to tour racing since I am now a professional instructor; however, I still feel I am close to my Olympic form.

TWO GENERAL TRAINING GUIDELINES

I have tried just about all training methods. Whenever I learn about a new method, I go right out and try it for a month or so in an effort to evaluate it. If this does nothing else, at least the change in training lifts my spirits for a brief period. I highly recommend to all young athletes that they also try new things, even if it is just for the variety.

However, from all this I have concluded that *what* or *when* one does the work is unimportant. *How* it is done is very important. As a rule of thumb, I would suggest here that the key word is *overtired*—how to do as much work as possible without getting overtired. Definite negative results of overtiredness are wasted time, disinterest, probable sickness, and a drop in the performance curve.

A second rule of thumb guide to successful training is avoiding *tension*. Again, how to do as much speed training as possible without becoming tense. I relate tension immediately to speed, since speedwork is essential in any training program and is the most likely type of training where tension will occur. If one runs or skis absolutely as fast as possible when he does his speed training, I say he is training himself to be tense, instead of developing speed. The kind of speed needed for an endurance sport is not blinding speed, but relaxed speed of quiet power.

This is a subtle thing, but very important. If it is left undiscussed with a young athlete, he may waste a whole season developing tension which does him no good at all, then he needs half of another season getting rid of it before he can start developing loose, relaxed speed.

Some athletes like to train alone, some in groups. Some twice a day, some three times, some once. Some athletes like to do mostly speed work, some like distance, some spend a lot of time on weights, some like roller skiing—whatever! I honestly believe it really doesn't matter; however, for the average individual, I would advise a little bit of everything and moderation. I think each person will eventually find his favorite types of training and he should use these most frequently.

But one shouldn't forget competition! Competition is not only the reason for doing the training in the first place, but it's also the fun part of athletics—or should be. Of course, all competitions don't end the way we want them to, but even these bad days can serve a useful purpose. Usually a weakness can be spotted and some training change made which might turn out to be of great value.

INDIVIDUAL PROGRAM ORGANIZATION

To this point, I have discussed training from an individual standpoint and I have mentioned two general guidelines with which to approach any training program. I would now like to overshadow all of this with one other training necessity: *organization*. By this I mean individual program organization on a seasonal and on a career basis. As I said earlier, what you specifically do in training is not, in my opinion, important. What is important is that you have things written down, both records of what you did and outlines of what you intend to do.

The Norwegians seem to be very good at this, particularly in their career set-up. For one thing, their whole country is very sports-minded. The skiing organization is basically set up around a club-team system instead of a school-team system as in our country. The significant difference here is that in the Norwegian system, no one individual is pushed to perform beyond his ability and/or potential. American school teams seem to be in many cases coached with only seasonal interests in mind, such as winning the area's championship at any cost. Along the route to these championships, there are many wasted athletes lying at the side of the track, if you will.

I think an individual who has a plan of attack for his career, plus a realistic program in outline form that will get him to that point, will tend to brainwash himself (in a positive way) into thinking that it is possible for him to "get there." This, of course, is half the battle!—and well worth the time it will take to write out such outlines. All through our lives we enter into contracts, and we are expected to accomplish whatever the contracts says we agreed to do. The above outlines for daily endeavor and the career plan are in a sense contracts one is writing with himself.

TOTALITY OF EXPERIENCE

by John Caldwell

A former coach of the US Nordic Ski Team ('65 to '72) and the author of
The *New* Cross-Country Ski Book, **John Caldwell has recently completed a book
on nordic training titled** Caldwell on Cross-Country, training and technique. **The
book will be published in the spring of '75 by The Stephen Greene Press of
Brattleboro, Vt. This article is based on material in the book.**

I'm a great believer in the totality of experience in training. In its very
broadest interpretation, totality of experience has many meanings but space and
time permit me to cover only two aspects of this idea.

We all talk about the limiting factors of exercise. For instance, we might
say that Athlete A could improve his performance if he could improve his oxygen
uptake. For the present, this is his limiting factor. Or, in the case of Athlete B,
his limiting factor is strength.

We might go on to detail special workouts for these athletes. For Athlete
A, we might prescribe a series of intense interval workouts in the hope that his
oxygen uptake would eventually improve. We might put Athlete B on weights
and strength exercises of various sorts.

All this is a straightforward approach and maybe it's the best we can do.
But I don't think so.

I agree with the physiologists who believe that the limiting factors of exercise, if there are any, all converge. In other words, the two athletes I mention
have more than single-effect problems. Athlete A is not slowing down (or going
into oxygen debt) simply because his oxygen uptake is not high enough. There
are other factors we might not be able to identify at this time, and perhaps still
other factors that we may never be able to identify. When an athlete slows during intense exercise, all his systems are converging, or causing the slowdown.

So what do you do for training? Of course, you keep at it, but you try to
make your training as similar to your event as possible. And by this I mean more
than just specificity exercises. In order to build strength for cross-country skiing,
ski-walking up hills with a pack on your back during a distance run or hike would
come near the top of my list. In this instance, all systems would be "go," so to
speak. They might all be in a state similar to that during an actual skiing competition. On the other hand, lifting weights would not appear as high on my list
for reasons which should be obvious.

Totality of experience also carries over into the athlete's everyday life.
There's more to life than just concentrating on one single purpose, no matter
what that purpose is. The athlete who is too single-minded about his training
and competition is going to have a very hard time of it, in my opinion.

There's always a need for relaxation, for other low-key interests, and a need for pointing to a job. No athlete I know can train and compete (as an amateur) for years in the United States without an eye to the future. If he feels uncertain about his future, or security, it will adversely effect his training and his competitive performances.

Unfortunately, some of the present day coaches and administrators have not been able to strike a balance here for the athlete. The result has been that many US athletes have quit or lost their effectiveness as racers.

John Caldwell (foreground) with US Ski Team members on their 10-day, 270-mile hike in 1970. (R. George)

2

Roller Skiing

by Lennart Strand

The year's training for a serious nordic racer starts long before the snow comes. In fact, unless the skier lives in a northern area where there's snow throughout most of the year, he'll likely spend more time in dry-land training than in actual training on snow. Roller skiing has become one of the most popular and effective avenues to dry-land conditioning for cross-country skiers.

Lennart Strand of Eskilstuna, Sweden is a nordic coach and skier. A journalist by profession, he's assistant managing editor of the Eskilstuna Courir and the senior European contributor to *Nordic World* magazine.

Sweden's Thomas Magnusson, the gold medalist in the 30-kilometer at the '74 world nordic skiing championships in Falun, Sweden in February, is completely convinced of the merits of roller skiing:

"Yes, it is excellent strength training for the arms, and the stomach and back muscles. Besides, it is good circulation training, as tests done here in Sweden have shown."

The Swedish world champion practices what he preaches: his summer training consists of 50 percent roller skiing.

Roller skiing is also considered to be one of the main explanations for the great advance which the East German skiers, most notably world champions Gerhard Grimmer and Gert-Dietmar Klause, have made in recent years.

Grimmer and Co. do many miles of roller skiing in the summertime, building themselves up in the arms specifically while at the same time gaining all-round body strength.

The rest of Europe as well now devotes a great deal of summer training time to roller skis. For example, in Norway you can see top skiers poling their way up one hill after another.

But it should also be stressed that there are skiers among the world's elite who hardly ski a meter on roller skis. Benny Södergren is a short-distance and relay specialist who is a member of the Swedish "A" team (a group of eight men, including Thomas Magnusson, which Sweden is concentrating on prior to the '76 Olympics at Innsbruck). Södergren does not at all approve of poling his way along the roads on roller skis:

"No, it becomes very tedious and does not suit me. I do it every so often, but not on a regular basis."

There are divided opinions, therefore, on the pleasure of roller skiing. But there is one thing which athletes and coaches alike agree on, and that is that roller skiing is fine strength training.

In this connection, there's one thing that's important to point out: the idea with roller skis should not be to use them in such a fashion that the activity resembles skiing as closely as possible.

To ski fast in winter, you need strong arm, stomach and back muscles. Roller skiing, therefore, should first and foremost be an activity for strengthening the aforementioned muscle groups. And the best way to do this is to use the double-pole technique. The diagonal technique should be used only now and then for variation, so the training does not get too dull and monotonous.

(Editor's Note: The above recommended approach to roller skiing differs with that of the US Ski Team. As explained in the next article, the US Ski Team uses the diagonal technique extensively with roller skiing.)

Of course, you can just as easily train the arm, stomach and back muscles in a weight lifting parlor, but sitting and tormenting the body in a weight lifting parlor does not suit everyone. Most skiers think it's more fun to roller ski. On roller skis you can combine "business with pleasure," as it were, and get out of doors as well.

Besides strength training, roller skiing also provides technique training to some extent. For example, you can work on polishing arm movement when you pole, letting the arms stretch out far behind the body and gliding out on the skis after each pole placement, just like you do on snow in the wintertime.

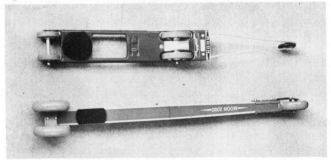

The two standard types of roller skis. (L. Strand)

What style of roller ski should you get? In general there are two different types on the market, one is short and the other is half-long. Tests in Sweden have shown that it does not make any great difference which type you use. Most roller skis have shown very good performance characteristics when used on smooth asphalt roads; the reliability in general was also very good.

The best thing to do is to try both types, if possible, before you decide which to get. Some think the shorter ones are better, while others think roller skiing is "more natural" on the somewhat longer wooden skis. But as indicated, the training effect is just as good on both types.

Regular roller skis can only be used effectively on paved roads. But there are special large-wheeled roller skis you can get for skiing on gravel and dirt roads —see above. *(Editor: The roller skis in the illustration are available from Eldar Hagen Sport, Hausmann Sgt., Oslo, Norway.)*

CONDITIONING, TECHNIQUE

by Steve Williams
Special Coach, US Ski Team

A graduate of Dartmouth College and the Yale Law School, Steve Williams was granted a two-year leave of absence from his teaching position at the Deerfield Academy in Deerfield, Mass. to assist the US Nordic Ski Team for the next two years leading up to the '76 Winter Olympics. An experienced coach and a former competitor, Steve, who is 27, has served as the US nordic program coordinator and assistant cross-country coach the past two years.

Roller skiing, while relatively new as a dry-land training technique, is becoming increasingly vital and, in fact, nearly essential to a total pre-season conditioning program for the serious cross-country skier. Athletes the world over are now spending a large portion of their off-season training time on roller skis, some as much as half their time (like world champion Thomas Magnusson of Sweden, for example). This year the members of the US Ski Team were expected to do 1200 kilometers of roller skiing before going on snow in early November. This figures out to an average of 50 kilometers, or usually three sessions, of roller skiing per week.

There is, however, disagreement as to the best way to use roller skis for training (*Nordic World*, July '74). Should a skier confine himself primarily to double poling or can he also gain from diagonal striding with the single-poling action?

While double poling does much for upper-torso development, the near exclusion of single sticking prevents the skier, in my opinion, from gaining the full possible benefits of roller skiing. This narrow view is most practised by the Norwegians, who only double pole, even on long tours (which has to limit the possible terrain they can use).

Most other nations don't accept this limitation of how to utilize roller skis, and train instead on roller skis just as they would on real skis. Sweden, for example, has developed specially-designed fiberglass tracks which are laid over miles of regular ski trails and terrain, and, through the use of roller skis, are skied just as in winter. The present philosophy of the US Ski Team is the same, except that we don't have the special over-land tracks. Our athletes are confined to paved roads, following them wherever they lead, and letting the terrain dictate the correct technique, just as on snow.

Cross-country skiing is a very difficult sport to train for because it requires total body conditioning—good pulmonary-cardiovascular efficiency and endurance upper torso strength, and explosive power in the legs. With one exception, the various requirements of cross-country can be met by a combination of conventional training techniques that focus on one or more individual areas (e.g., running, hill bounding with or without poles, weight training, and even double poling on roller skis). However, only diagonal-stride roller skiing allows a skier to work on the recovery phase of the kick—the powerful swing and drive of the "recovery" leg forward which produces a strong glide.

MECHANICS OF THE KICK IN SKIING

The most misapplied, or at least misunderstood, and hence vague and meaningless term in cross-country, has to be the word "kick." The kick and principle of forward propulsion in skiing is usually explained as a downward and backward push with the *stationary* (initially forward) leg—which propels the body forward onto the other (initially trailing) leg—*recovery leg*—which has recovered to its normal, balanced position beneath the skier's center of gravity.

It is physically impossible that a backward push with a smooth-bottomed, uncleated ski alone produces much forward thrust (despite what the "scooter" theory suggests). This is not to deny the necessity of a strong downward push (actually an isometric contraction) by the stationary leg, but that is primarily to stabilize the body and set a fixed fulcrum around which the forward thrust of the recovery leg originates. This move is made off the ball of the foot.

In the same manner as a soccer player kicking a ball, the kick in skiing is realized when the skier strongly swings or kicks his trailing (recovery) leg forward. But instead of sitting back and letting the foot rise in a follow-through as the kicker would, the skier keeps his head forward and his center of gravity above his recovery knee as it swings forward, riding ahead on the now-gliding ski, the knee never getting behind the heel. The knee presses forward—with the center of gravity always above it, but with the heel *never* getting ahead. In other words, the knee is always in a dynamic, forward position.

Thus, a kick is really a two-legged movement, one which roller skiing can help develop technically and train a skier for physically. No other dry-land activity involves the same type of movement or range of motion, taxing the hip flexors and quadriceps in the drive forward. In Figure 1 below, Martha Rockwell has just begun her kick with her kight leg. Notice the muscle contraction in the right quadricep.

THE BENEFITS OF DOUBLE POLING

The attention given to the diagonal stride here in our discussion is not to underplay the importance of the double-pole. As mentioned earlier, a good, vigorous double-pole, with or without a kick, is very effective for the development of upper torso and arm strength, as well as endurance.

By using the double-pole, the skier can also learn the helpful effect of momentum. Once a skier has built up momentum, it is easier to maintain it than to regain it after slowing down. In using the more demanding and difficult double-pole, the skier has the chance to mentally condition himself to be tough and work on maintaining his momentum, something he can carry over onto snow. Bicycling in rolling hill terrain illustrates and teaches the same thing.

Figure 1:
Perennial US
women's champion—
Martha Rockwell.

As with the diagonal stride, a skier can work on his technique with the double-pole—hands perpendicular to the shoulders, poles parallel to torso angle, and the initial thrust (*compression*) coming from the upper body merely falling (pushing) over onto the hands, as the arms isometrically (without movement) contract with the hands positioned still perpendicular to the upper torso (Figure 2). The knees do bend a little to absorb the downward compression and weight of the torso.

Only then, with his back almost parallel to the ground, does the skier push to the rear with his arms. If he leaves his arms over his head (compresses his upper body too fast), the skier loses the mechanical advantage of having work done by mere body weight falling on his poles. Furthermore, he assumes a very mechanically inefficient position of having to pull his arms almost 180° from over his head to the rear.

The kick for the double-pole is the same in principle to the kick in the diagonal, except that it's all done off one leg, so to speak. The skier does rely to some extent on the "scooter" effect of pushing back with the kicking leg, but the real forward thrust comes out of the recovery swing and drive forward by that leg. The more completely the skier transfers his weight up onto the stationary leg as he "winds up" for the kick, the more powerful the kick will be (Figure 3).

A DANGER FOR THE BEGINNER

Much attention has been given here to technique because if an experienced skier makes a conscientious effort while roller skiing, significant improvements in technique can be made. And, of course, these improvements should carry over to snow.

Roller skiing is limited, though, in how much it can do for the beginning skier. While roller skis are tremendous for conditioning and technical modifications, they are not a good device for introducing a beginner to the sport.

The novice can get the idea for a forward driving kick and glide on roller skis, but only with constant coaching should any but the most athletic novice attempt to go beyond this introductory stage.

Every skier has to make a technical adjustment when roller skiing since the recovery roller ski is not directed or guided ahead by a track as in snow. Also, once the roller ski has its wheels on the ground it cannot be slid laterally to get it under the skier's center of gravity. Thus, the skier has to make a conscious physical adjustment to make sure as he recovers his roller ski that it's headed straight ahead and is under him. This results in the novice not extending enough or fully transferring his weight from one ski to the other (the winter-time track straddler who pushes instead of driving his ski ahead).

The experienced skier, of course, does have enough practice and trained balance to be able to relax and fully extend with each kick, even if he does not go perfectly straight. Besides, his kick is so conditioned that it is fairly well directed anyway. (In Figure 1, notice Martha Rockwell's ski "straightening itself out.")

The novice is limited further by a rightful fear of falling on the pavement. This works to limit his relaxation, and hence his extension and weight transfer. The novice is hesitant to assume a correct, forward, dynamic body position, so he never attains enough forward momentum to fully extend. Nor does he use his poles correctly. The pole should be planted aggressively, always at an effective

Figure 2. "Only then . . . does the skier push to the rear with his arms."

Figure 3. The more complete the "wind up," the more powerful the kick.

"attack" angle towards the rear, so the skier only pushes back. The novice will use his poles more for balance than propulsion, planting the poles perpendicular and further out to the side as "outriggers".

Thus, roller skiing, while good for technique training by an experienced skier, is not advisable to any great extent for the beginning skier since there are factors (no tracks, the pavement, etc.) which make it actually harder to roller ski well than snow ski. Unless there is constant viewing by a coach, it is just too easy for the novice to develop and drill home bad habits using roller skis.

HOW TO TRAIN WITH ROLLER SKIS

Discussion thus far has centered on technique. This is not intended to over-shadow the tremendous training (i.e., conditioning) benefits possible with roller skiing, but only to highlight the fact the technique training is also a very real possibility with roller skis.

Roller skiing is skiing's most closely related dry-land training activity because, simply, it *is* skiing. It completely simulates or mimics the real thing and has the same physical demands. This is not to say one should exclusively roller ski, because as with any physical activity, improvement is gained from an overload principle. The only real way to increase capacity is to push against present maximum tolerance, and the event alone without supplementation does not make sufficient demands on the entire physiological system to gain maximum improvement.

Roller skiing is done on paved roads, wherever they're to be found and wherever they lead. The terrain encountered dictates to some extent the technique used. Incidentally, the roller skier observes the same rules of the road as runners: go against the traffic and stay as much to the side of the road as possible. Through intelligent route planning, you can usually find good, seldom-travelled roads. Naturally, you should avoid roads which have heavy traffic.

Long gradual, or even medium-grade, uphills are particularly good for roller skiing. Almost all roller skis are faster with more carry than snow skis, and the increased gravitational resistance when skiing uphill adds enough resistance to make either diagonal or double poling an overload situation, and particularly good.

Long tours of up to 40-50 kilometers are not unheard of, though tours of that length should only be done by the best skiers in top physical condition. The usual is in the order of 10-20 kilometers of non-stop, steady-state roller skiing.

Specific intense workouts—tempo (race-speed, full recovery) or interval (repeated efforts with moderate recovery, pulse 120)—can also be done on roller skis. The same principles would apply here as in foot running. The shorter and faster the repeated efforts, the less attention can be paid to technique, and the more likely only double poling will be used.

One of our favorite workouts is over an approximately 300-meter, gradually steepening uphill (or whatever distance takes a skier at full speed one minute, 20 seconds to ski) done as a series of intervals. Hopefully, the coast downhill to the start will get the athlete's pulse down to 120. Twenty of these intervals makes a very tough 40-45 minute workout.

A note of caution regarding roller skiing downhills. Experience and confidence will dictate to the skier what hills he can ski down, but discretion should

Tours up to 40-50 kilometers are possible, but should only be done by skiers in top physical condition. (Robert George)

also be a factor. While long pants and gloves are good protection for low-speed falls (and recommended), they may not be much help in a fall at high speed. The scrape and resulting scab from a big fall can actually restrict training for a while. A skier should not be too proud to take his skis off and walk down steeper hills, particularly if there are corners in the road or traffic.

SELECTING ROLLER SKIS

There are about three or four brands of roller skis presently available in North America and without recommending any one brand, I would like to briefly discuss the essential characteristics of a good ski.

All roller skis work on the basis of a ratchet wheel or some brake device in front which is necessary to hold the ski stationary so that a kick can be initiated. It is this same brake effect that encourages a "scooter" push backward. The further the binding (specifically the ball of the skier's foot) is behind the brake or ratchet wheel, the better. There is less friction, reducing the capacity of the skier to push back; therefore, the more forward his drive has to be.

In selecting a pair of roller skis, one should carefully consider the weight of the ski. The heavier the ski, the harder it will be for the skier to fully extend onto his gliding ski (which pulls his trailing leg up in the air) because the weight will work to hold the ski on or near the ground, pulling the skier back so that he is not up on top of his gliding ski. This reduces his recovery drive forward on his next stride, all of which means shortened strides.

The roller ski also should be low enough to the ground (approximately 3") so that the pole plant on pavement places the basket on the same plane relative to the skier's foot as it would be in snow. Longer poles should not have to be used, but if you find that the arm swing has to be modified (probably shorter and lower) from normal when you're roller skiing, change the poles—or skis.

The balance of the roller skis and their tracking ability are also worth considering. The front of the ski should hang a little so that the front wheel is the first part of the ski to contact the ground. This gives the skier something of a feeler or finder so that the recovery is ahead. Also, it is important that the skis run straight, either singly in the recovery glide, or together on flats or downhills.

The same poles as used in skiing (hopefully the same length) can be used for roller skiing, though use of poles with regular steel tips should be avoided. Many models now come with tungsten steel or carbide tips, which stay sharper much longer, and there are carbide tip adapters (collars) which can be slipped on over the pole tips. Otherwise, snow-tire studs could be welded on the ends. The point is, however, that you need some type of extra-strong tip on your poles when roller skiing.

The pole straps should not be attached to the top of the pole as with alpine poles, but should be attached down off the top-side of the handle, leaving a nob on top. This nob is essential for a complete weight transfer as it allows a full extension of the arm behind. The skier can let go of the handle and open up his hand, yet keep control over the pole in the cradle formed by his thumb and forefinger.

Roller skis are still not widely available in the US. Isolated ski shops have them and occasional individuals have access to roller skis directly from Europe.

(Editor's Note: Three US importers of the popular Bergans roller ski are: Janoy Incorporated, 2000 E. Center Circle Drive, Minneapolis, Minn. 55441; Akers Ski, Andover, Maine, 04216; and Nordic Trails, 255 Jayne Avenue, Suite 301, Oakland, Calif. 94610.)

ROAD SHOCK

One problem with roller skiing is road shock. The skier is continually trying to make his poles stick in the pavement, but unlike in snow, there is no give, thus no absorption of the shock of the pole plant. This can lead to sore elbows (similar to tennis elbow) or even back problems.

At present there is little that can be done to counter this except perhaps restricting training to smooth, newer tarred roads. Moon, a Swedish company which manufactures roller skis and poles (only a few of which are seen in the US), has developed a spring-loaded, collar-like device on the tips of poles which does give a skier some shock absorption.

Gloves can be worn not only for protection from falls but also to prevent blistering from road shock.

The same boots and bindings are used with roller skis as with regular skis. Use bolts that go through the entire ski when mounting bindings on a metal roller ski (such as the Bergans ski), rather than placing screws in the top only. Screws will slip easily. Use lock washers to counter the loosening effect of road vibration.

MAINTENENCE

The biggest problem with most roller skis, at least the Bergans model, is that the screws on the hubs, which hold the tires on, often loosen due to road vibration and fall out, leaving the tire to fall off. You should either check these screws regularly or epoxy them in permanently. Also, regularly check the nuts which hold the wheels on the axles. Make sure there are washers with the nuts (not lock washers).

The wheels should be oiled with the same regularity as one would oil bicycle wheel axles. Excessive oiling is dangerous since oil, while lubricating and minimizing friction between surfaces, also picks up dirt and grime which could do more serious damage.

As mentioned earlier, pole tips should be extra-tough. They should also be sharpened when dull.

3

On
Snow

by Steve Williams

The period of transition from dry-land training to actual skiing is very important and should be well planned and deliberate.

This is the time when a skier tries to channel all his work of the summer and fall into the real thing for the winter racing season. Foot running, biking and skiing are quite different activities and do not necessarily compliment each other. As a skier makes the transition, he must be careful so that the time and effort he has put into pre-season training is not wasted.

This is also the time when a skier forms many of the habits which will characterize his skiing technique throughout the year. The skier should concentrate particularly, therefore, on good technique during this period and phasing out bad habits.

IMPORTANCE OF TECHNIQUE

At this point, it's worthwhile to stress why a skier should concern himself with technique. A good "technical" skier is one who channels most of his energy and effort "down the track"—the only direction which will get him closer to the finish line—thereby getting the most effective, efficient and economical use of his body's capacity. Every skier gets tired in a race and as he does, his concentration weakens and he has less ability to exert strict conscious control over his movements. Hence, his movements will become those which are more natural and fundamental. If a skier is not a good technical skier, his movements will degenerate to "scrambling" or "thrashing and bashing," with a substantial portion of his energy being diverted from propelling the skier "down the track" to extraneous, wasted motions (sideways or up and down). The better a skier's technique and the more ingrained it is into his subconscious, the better (and longer) he will be able to maintain efficient and effective use of whatever energy he has without wasting it on unnecessary movements. And there is no better time to start (or continue) conditioning a skier for this than in the transitional period before the pressure of frequent races starts with the resulting increased emphasis on speed training.

Specifically, a skier should spend a great deal of time on snow in the transitional period doing distance training—while always maintaining a conscious effort to ski technically well. How much distance? The more miles skied, the more natural the technique becomes. One must, however, be cautious and not overdo the technique part of technique training by just going in stop-action, slow motion. Ski hard, but *within* your technique.

One thing to remember in technique training is that "technique" encompasses *all* the movements that carry a skier around a cross-country course, be it double poling, hill running, herringboning, skiing or skating around turns, going over bumps—not just single sticking along a flat. True, the single stick, diagonal stride is the basis of all cross-country technique, but too often it is concentrated upon to the exclusion of all other skiing movements.

When skiers are skiing "technique," they should concentrate on all their skiing movements within a given time span as opposed to a particular skiing movement, which is usually single sticking. Ski non-slow for a given time— through any type of terrain used. It is fine to ski on a golf course to concentrate on single sticking as long as the skier does not ski to a corner, let up, walk around the corner, and then resume skiing.

DEVELOPING BETTER BALANCE

Included in the early season transitional program should be at least two 20-minute sessions of "no-pole" skiing. However, "no-pole" skiing can be overdone. If done in moderation it helps a skier get his balance on the skis without having poles to utilize as crutches or supports. Thus, when the skier picks up his poles, he has the balance to extend completely on the gliding (forward travelling) ski and to get maximum benefit of his forward drive. And he is able to use his poles strictly for forward propulsion without having to stick them out to the side for balance.

A skier should not abandon dry-land training as soon as he starts skiing. During the first seven to 10 days of on-snow training a skier should continue on a full skeleton version of his respiratory (foot) workouts. He should take two, if not three, short foot running workouts which demand near maximum respiratory and cardiovascular exertion. A typical workout would be three to four five-minute interval runs. By doing this many full-effort exertions in the first week (since three is the maximum number of full-effort workouts that should be done in any week anyway), a skier then leaves himself free to totally concentrate on his technique, as there is no need to reach maximum oxygen uptake during his skiing workouts. However, again a word of caution against doing the skiing too slow.

FOOT RUNNING TO MAINTAIN OXYGEN UPTAKE LEVEL

After the first seven to 10 days, a skier can phase out some, but not all, of the dry-land workouts while increasing to a full schedule of skiing workouts. It is doubtful that a cross-country skier will be in as good "pure" respiratory and cardiovascular condition in the winter as he is at the peak of his dry-land training. Skiing is not as fast a movement as foot running and more of a skier's energy is expended on the muscular act of setting and driving off his skis. Thus, less of his capacity is expended on strict high respiratory exertion. Consequently, a skier's maximum oxygen uptake will tend to slacken to a certain extent. This is not to say a skier is not in as good condition in February as in November, but only that this particular aspect of condition will decline slightly. Thus, a skier should continue foot running throughout the winter with at least one full-effort interval running workout a week (in addition to at least two high intensity skiing workouts) to maintain his speed and his oxygen uptake as near peak level as possible.

As for the skiing workouts, once a skier has (hopefully) many miles from the first seven to 10 days behind him and as the racing season approaches, he should reduce the number of distance workouts and substitute interval and tempo training for most of the distance. Since the number of foot running workouts is also reduced at this same time after the first week, it is necessary to have near maximum exertions on skis as well as on foot. It is then that a skier is able to combine all aspects of his training into the final product—skiing technically well and yet going at his maximum rate. All the work up until then has been to maintain one's respiratory and cardiovascular capacity at as high a level as possible while he waits for his technique and efficiency to develop up to his capacity to exert.

TRACK SETTING

by Steve Williams

The importance of a good track for effective cross-country ski training cannot be over-stated. It is nearly impossible for a young, learning skier to acquire the balance he needs if he is not skiing in a good track, or for a good skier to maintain his balance.

If there is no track to give direction to a skier's forward drive with his "recovery" leg, he will expend unnecessary effort. Furthermore, because of the uncertainty with no track of exactly where the forward driving ski is going and whether or not it will be under him, a skier has a natural and instinctive tendency to hold back on his forward drive, thereby not completing this drive and reaping all the benefit of the effort he has put into it.

With this failure to complete the forward drive, the skier does not and cannot fully extend onto the gliding ski. Consequently, to hold his balance due to a shorter glide, the skier drops the rear leg to the track, well behind the front foot. This then reduces the effectiveness of his next forward drive as he not only has to drag the ski along the track from behind himself to in front, but he then can only push the ski ahead, as opposed to having had a complete extension from which he can drive his "recovery" leg forward freely.

Obviously, it is beneficial and indeed essential to a skier's proper development to have a good track where he can acquire balance and the feeling of a complete extension and glide. And it is not good "strategy" for a coach to have his skiers train on courses fit for mountain goats even if that were the only type of courses his skiers were to compete on. A skier with good balance on one ski at a time is always at an advantage over the shuffler.

With the case for good tracks thus briefly presented, I would go on to urge the use of a track sled to set tracks as opposed to actually stamping them in with skis. Not only is it hard to keep tracks an appropriate or consistent distance apart (5½"-6") when they are set by skis, but tracks set in fresh snow tend to set up "railroad tracks," two packed-down ridges with soft snow on both sides. A ski can easily slip off such a track (usually to the inside), thus breaking the track down.

Another good reason to use a track sled is to save time. It is far less time-consuming for a coach to have a track sled to pull around a course behind a snowmobile than to have his team waste a lot of valuable practice time stamping in a track.

Below is a drawing and building instructions for a good all-purpose track sled. This sled was designed by Sven Johanson, a long-time coach of the US Army Biathlon Team.

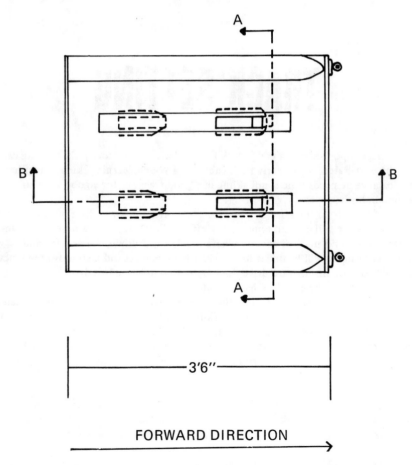

FORWARD DIRECTION

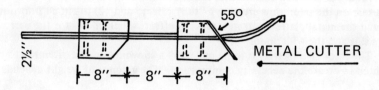

SECTION BB

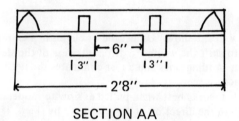

SECTION AA

BUILDING THE SLED

Materials: 36"x32"x¾" sheet of plywood, one pair of old skis, eight hardwood blocks (four of them should be 8"x3"x2½"), two 6"x3" metal plates, eight 6"x¼" stove bolts, two dozen 1½"x¼" bolts, and 32 nuts and washers, Elmer's glue, and two rings and hangers.

Step 1—To bend the plywood, relieve by saw to ½" in depth every ½" for 6-8" from your chosen front of the sled.

Step 2—Cut the skis to desired length; use the 1½"x¼" bolts to attach the skis to the plywood.

Step 3—Bend the plywood, by bracing the front of the sled off the ground and weighting it. Place glue in the slots to aid the holding of the bend. Allow 24 hours to dry.

Step 4—Cut blocks to desired shape and size (8"x2½"x3" and modify as shown). Find the center line of your sled. Three inches to either side of the center line will be the inside edge of the runners (or blocks). Use the 6"x¼" stove bolts (recessed) to attach the runners and above holding blocks to the sled.

Step 5—Make 3"x3" slots in front of the fore-runners to allow the metal plates to be slid through and fastened. These holes allow snow accumulating in front of the fore-runners to funnel out.

Step 6—Paint sled desired color (two to three coats). Fiberglassing the bottom is well worth the additional cost in the lengthened life of the sled.

Step 7—Attach rings and hangers for pulling as shown.

A couple of modifications that might be considered are: 1) to build sides and a rear on the sled; thus creating a "tub" effect; and 2) to cut all four runners and the metal plates to create a tapered effect, which allows for the narrow racing skis and the wider boot.

The track sled (setter) is to be pulled by a snowmobile and often has to be weighted to create the necessary compression. The amount of weight depends

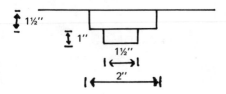

on the consistency of the snow. Using sand or chains in a grain bag works well as it is then easy to shift the weight to different areas of the sled or change the amount of weight. Adding sides and a rear eliminates the need for straps to hold the weights in place.

The track sled works best when pulled at slow to moderate speeds. The sled should be run in the direction of the course to be skied. If steep hills present a problem, this can be circumvented by running the sled down the hills.

One or two skiers should follow behind the sled to smooth up the track. This is also the rationale behind four smaller runners as opposed to two long runners on the sled.

This sled will work in the widest range of snow conditions, as it not only can compress soft snow, but also cut a track in fairly hard packed snow as well. If the fore-runners were altered so they duplicated the design of the rear runners, (i.e., without the metal plates or holes) this sled would do a smoother job of setting tracks in soft (new) snow, but would have difficulty compressing a track in hard (old) snow. The wisdom of making such an adjustment needs to be weighed against the anticipated type of snow cover during the year.

If this sled is adjusted so as to make it purely a compression sled, there is another sled, purely a cutting sled, that can be obtained from Haugen, Inc., Henshaw, Woburn, Massachusetts 01801. Such a sled could also be built, but this would require an excellent sheet metal worker. Essentially, this sled is a frame with 2-3" strips of sheet metal 6" apart connected by a frame.

4

The Europeans

Europe has dominated nordic ski racing ever since the sport began. Statistics released by the FIS (the international skiing federation) after the '74 world nordic championships showed that Norway is the leading nation in total nordic medals won in Olympic and world championship competition. Norway has won a total of 57 gold medals, 52 silver medals and 50 bronze medals for a total of 1,132 points (these statistics include ski jumping and the nordic combined). The next three countries, with their respective medal and point totals, are: Finland—40, 48, 37 for 889 points; Sweden—33, 29, 39 for 727 points; and the USSR—33, 25, 25 for 580 points. The US and Canada are 14th and 16th on the list with nine points and one point respectively. Neither country has ever won an Olympic or world championship medal in nordic racing.

The Scandinavian countries and the Soviet Union have been the leading European nations in cross-country skiing. But the new power on the scene is East Germany, which won the majority of the medals in the '74 world championships. The man who has built the East German team is Hannes Braun, the head coach and developer of such outstanding East German racers as Gerhard Grimmer, Dieter Meinel, Gert-Dietmar Klause and others.

In nordic skiing as in other sports, the East Germans are usually regarded as being secretive about their training methods. But in October of '74 coach Braun visited a Swedish training camp where he freely answered questions of leading Swedish skiers on the East German program. In the first article in this chapter, Lennart Strand reports on that question-and-answer session.

Interval training is used in cross-country skiing as in other endurance sports. Interestingly, however, straight interval training has never received the kind of widespread acceptance in nordic skiing that it has in distance running and swimming. In the second article in this chapter, David (Dalle) Johansson, Thomas Magnusson's coach, answers the "intervals vs. distance" question.

The final article in this chapter, and the longest one in the book, is by Rolf Kjaernsli, one of Norway's leading nordic coaches. An assistant nordic coach on both the '68 and '72 Norwegian Winter Olympic teams, coach Kjaernsli (pronounced *Charn-slee*) writes on "Peaking for Racing." But his article includes a lengthy and highly-informative description (complete with a graph and charts) of the Norwegian year-round program. He even shows how the program can be scaled down for junior and female skiers.

Incidentally, coach Kjaernsli is no stranger to North America, having been employed for five years by the Canadian Ski Association to promote nordic skiing and instruct coaches. He now lives in Lillehammer, Norway.

EAST GERMAN PROGRAM

by Lennart Strand

"I'm sorry that everybody thinks that there is so much secretiveness behind our training methods. One of the reasons behind our success is the very good contact in our country between chief coaches from different sports. After every big event, all our coaches from the different sports meet and discuss and learn from each other's success or failure."

The man speaking is East German national cross-country ski coach Hannes Braun. In October of this year, he visited a Swedish national training camp in Rattvik, Dalarna, where the Swedish ski stars had a chance to ask him whatever they wanted. Mr. Braun answered in Swedish, a language he knows quite well after having attended many training camps in northern Sweden.

THE YEAR-ROUND PROGRAM

One of the first questions he was asked was: How do you plan a training year?

Mr. Braun gave a detailed answer, using the year before the '74 world championships in Falun, Sweden, as an example.

"January-March was race season as usual. April we spent in Sweden in a combined race and training camp. Around April 20 we went home to East Germany for holidays and individual training. Many went to school, others worked. Now was also the time to take care of any injuries.

"In May we went to the Soviet Union for a 16-day training camp. But we did nothing hard, mostly alpine skiing, walks in the mountains, and so on. We call it active rest.

"In June we started going harder again. Not too much distance, approximately 10 sessions every week. Also we did athletics (track and field) and differend kinds of games.

"Therefore, month to month, from January to June, we did more and more distance work while the tempo eased off.

"In July the skiers had a three-week active-rest holiday with their families. In August we had a camp near Berlin where we also did some canoeing and soccer. After this we trained at home before going to a three-week camp where we had different kinds of races. The men, for instance, had two roller ski races, one 15-kilometer and one 50-kilometer. Also, they had a cross-country foot race over 10 kilometers.

"After this camp, the skiers had an active rest at their respective homes and then it was off to Murmansk in the northern Soviet Union for three weeks on snow. After that, three weeks at home and then back on snow again. And then it was December and race season, with our nationals at the end of the month.

East Germany's Gerhard Grimmer, 50-kilometer champion and the outstanding male racer at the '74 world championships. (L. Strand)

"Our heavy workouts are mostly done during training camps. During race season we shorten the workouts. We don't do any of the classic interval training, running so many minutes on a track or in hills. We think more favorably of the natural interval, the cross-country way.

"The reason we don't do classic interval training is because it easily develops anaerobic products in the muscles, which is bad for the muscles."

He was asked what kind of strength training the East German skiers did.

"We do calisthenics in general. We don't use barbells and things like that, especially Gerhard Grimmer is against these. (Grimmer is the East German superstar, world champion and a top international racer for many years.)

"We do calisthenics for a total of one hour at different stations. We work out for four minutes at one station, rest 30 seconds, then do four minutes at another station and so on. But we take it easy so that we don't build up any anaerobic products in the muscles.

"As a matter of fact, during training periods we never do any maximal training. We go at maximum intensity only during races. The important thing in training is to go at the right tempo (pace). Training too long and at too tough a pace tends to weaken the athlete instead of strengthening him. Younger athletes often go too long and too hard. The problem is to find the right level of training for each individual. And this is why the athlete needs to have good communication with his coach."

ROLLER SKIING

How about your roller-ski training? Mr. Braun was asked.

"In June, for example, the men roller skied 25 kilometers at each session while the foot-running sessions were between 10 and 20 kilometers. During the fall we cover longer and longer distances. Seventy to 80 percent of the time is spent on roller skis."

Do you have individual programs?

"East German coaches draw up a year-long plan covering 12 months. In this you have everything—intensity, distances, percentage of roller skiing, cross-country running and so on. Every athlete also has his own personal program, but this is as close as possible to the general plan."

How about physical tests?

"No, East German athletes don't like these. And it's the coaches who decide what the athlete shall do, by the way, not the doctor or the physiologist. But, of course, we keep a close eye on our athletes with physiological controls every other month."

Do your athletes eat any special food?

"Ordinary food is good. But it is not enough, so we take vitamin C all year around. During the heavy training periods, the athletes also need extra protein, but apart from that, ordinary home-cooked food is best."

INTERVALS VS. DISTANCE
by David (Dalle) Johansson

Intervals or distance?

How many times have I been asked that question? Now as always the answer is the same: both intervals and distance! There should be variation in training.

Dealing with intervals first, there are different ways you can train. You can do straight out intervals on a circular track, you can do them on a hill (it should not be too steep), you can do intervals on a bog or swamp that is not too soft, or you can do natural intervals. By the latter I mean that, for example, when you run 10 kilometers over hilly terrain and maintain the same speed, then every hill that you go over is an interval effort.

Distance or quantity training has been overdone during recent years—at least as far as I am concerned. Not by everyone, but by all too many. Common sense tells me that if I run or ski at the same speed up to five, six or seven hours a day, then later on it has to be difficult to change tempo. And no matter what the situation, you *have* to be able to ski fast when the time for competition comes. If I get my body used to a comfortable tempo, it stands to reason the body has to react negatively if called upon to go faster.

Thomas Magnusson, who is coached by David Johansson, en route to victory in the 30-kilometer at the '74 world championships. (L. Strand)

After having had the privilege of observing and assisting with Thomas Magnusson's training for six years, I think I am able to say that it is his fine blend of the different training methods which has made him so good.

Thomas does not make a muddle of it. Proper training is simple, but *very* laborious. When Thomas came to Delsbo as a junior, he did somewhat more intervals than he has done in recent years. He even did lactic acid (or oxygen debt) training several times a week, mostly in the fall.

Nowadays Thomas does very little straight interval training, but he runs and skis at a very fast, steady tempo over hilly terrain in his distance training. This gives him an excellent natural interval effect.

As most who follow nordic skiing know, Thomas has one of the toughest training programs of all time. Can Thomas train even harder, many ask. No, I do not think so. He set up his five-year plan in an ideal manner. He has increased his training from year to year, both in length (number of hours) and in tempo. Now he has reached the peak and the objective is to maintain his training at that level, which he is doing.

PEAKING FOR RACING

by Rolf Kjaernsli
Assistant Nordic Coach, '68 and '72 Norwegian Olympic Team

A question which is all-important to any serious cross-country racer is how to "get there when it counts." In other words, how does one peak for racing?

I do not think any coach should be dogmatic about this. More than any other aspect of training, peaking for racing requires an *individual* approach. The coach must know the skier, his background and previous training, and the way he reacts both mentally and physically to a "gearing up" effort.

However, some general points could perhaps be made. First, any peak must be built on a solid foundation of long-distance (quantity) training. The broader the foundation, the higher the peak may reach. This foundation is the result of a long and gradual process. From year to year the skier will raise the level of his platform (foundation), and so make possible a peak "soaring into the skies."

Against this it could be argued that there have been cases where skiers who have been ill or injured for weeks in the crucial fall building-up period still have succeeded in reaching a peak in February. Yes, but these skiers have all had a considerable background, with years of training and racing behind them. So the level of their platform was already high when they started a "crash" program to get there in February. And, what is worth noticing, their peak attained by this crash method was never of long duration; whereas racers with a solid, gradual build-up can win the first and last race of the season, and still have a "super-peak" in the middle.

It would take too long here to deal with how training is planned week by week around the year. But these charts from three training camps for the Norwegian national team (men) this fall will give you an idea how our top skiers train:

CHART ONE

Aug. 5—Mon.		Distance training	1 hr. 45 min.
Aug. 6—Tues.	1)	Distance training	2 hr. 15 min.
	2)	Roller skiing	45-65 min.
Aug. 7—Wed.		Distance training	5 hr.
Aug. 8—Thurs.	1)	Distance training (with two interval sections, 10-15 min. each)	2 hr. 5 min.
	2)	Roller skiing, hard	35-40 min.
	3)	Soccer	1 hr.
Aug. 9—Fri.	1)	Distance training	3 hr. 35 min.
	2)	Roller skiing	1 hr. 5 min.
Aug. 10—Sat.		Easy distance training (natural interval	1 hr. 45 min.

CHART TWO

Sept. 2—Mon.		Natural interval training	1 hr. 55 min.
Sept. 3—Tues.	1)	Distance training	3-3¼ hr.
	2)	Roller skiing	1-1¼ hr
			4 hr. 30 min.
Sept. 4—Wed.	1)	Distance training	2-2½ hr.
	2)	Interval training	1 hr.
			3 hrs. 30 min.
Sept. 5—Thurs.	1)	Distance training	2 hr. 5 min.
	2)	Roller skiing	50 min.
	3)	Soccer	1 hr.
			3 hr. 55 min.
Sept. 6—Fri.	1)	Distance training	2 hr. 35 min.
		Interval training (2 long stretches)	30 min.
	2)	Roller skiing	1 hr.
			4 hr. 5 min.
Sept. 7—Sat.		Distance training	1 hr. 40 min.

CHART THREE

Sept. 30—Mon.	1)	Distance training	2-3½ hr.
	2)	Roller skiing	1¼-1½ hr.
	3)	Volleyball	<u>45 min.</u>
			4-5¾ hr.
Oct. 1—Tues.	1)	Distance/Interval training	2-3¼ hr.
	2)	Roller skiing	1¼-1½ hr.
	3)	Volleyball	<u>45 min.</u>
			4-5½ hr.
Oct. 2—Wed.	1)	Distance training	3 hr.
	2)	Interval/Distance/Roller skis	<u>1-1¼ hr.</u>
			4-4¼ hr.
Oct. 3—Thurs.	1)	Distance training (some did 1-2 10-15 min. interval sections)	1¾-2¼ hr.
	2)	Natural interval	1¼ hr.
	3)	Volleyball	<u>45 min.</u>
			3¾-4¼ hr.
Oct. 4—Fri.	1)	Distance training	2 hr. 30 min.

November will be full of skiing at a fairly moderate pace. Some team members will train up to 140 hours during the month, but note that at least two-thirds of this is easy skiing (skiing for mileage).

A guide-line for further work is to intensify the training as the racing season approaches. Actual hours spent training will be less, but there will be more interval work and some oxygen debt training. Note: only *some* oxygen debt training, and this only a few weeks before the racing season starts. Norwegian training philosophy for cross-country skiing does not emphasize anaerobic work during training. One should, however, be aware that Norwegian skiers race more than their North American counterparts early in the season (e.g., December) and thus get some oxygen debt training in these early races.

A common mistake: When you feel "good," when the uphills are easy and the whole race a lark, then you think that *now*, "now I shall really make it," and you start training harder than ever in order to "beat the world"—only to be bitterly disappointed to find that in the next race you feel empty, sluggish, and powerless.

When you feel good, it is a sign that you are on your way towards a peak. Or you may already be there. This buoyancy of spirit and surplus of physical energy should be nursed and cherished like an infant child—not broken down by heedless spending of energy. An athlete on his way up to the peak is robust and can subject himself to strenuous efforts; but when he "is there," and especially when he has been there for some time and may approach the point of toppling over, then he must show some careful husbandry of his energy.

One of Norway's top skiers, Odd Martinsen, the world's fastest relay racer.
(L. Strand)

Frequent and tough racing calls for less training—easy going at a moderate pace. Even in the racing season a long-distance workout per week should be kept up, but the skier should not push himself too much in these workouts. There should be some skiing for fun.

If races are few and over short distances, harder training must be done, of course, to keep up strength and stamina. As racing schedules vary from skier to skier, and from country to country, it would be unwise to set up a standard weekly training program for the racing season. Such a standardized program might do more harm than good.

You may experience that the peak fails to show up in spite of long and steady training. The time has then come to sit down and analyze your training.

Have you been doing the same kind of training, same amount of hours and same intensity for weeks on end? If the hours of training have been many but the intensity low, there is reason to believe that you should intensify your training by doing higher speed, shorter workouts (more interval and oxygen-debt training). If, on the other hand, the intensity of your training has been high all along and you still feel a long way "off," you might find it profitable to slow down and *rest* more.

Of these two situations the former is by far the easier to remedy. When realizing that he is "behind schedule," an experienced skier on a solid platform will know how many days/weeks of a "crash" program he will need to get onto that peak. The period and effort needed will vary from individual to individual. Laboratory tests performed under reliable conditions may be of help, but for most skiers the way they *feel* will be the main guideline.

In the latter of the two situations mentioned above, the gun-powder has already been burnt. There is nothing to "go on," as the skier has tried to take a shortcut by striving for the peak without a solid foundation of long-distance training. He has gone bankrupt by trying to reach success in a hurry.

Rest is important during the build-up period, and equally so during the racing season. When in good shape you may feel that rest is unnecessary, but it is imperative that body and mind should relax between the battles.

In the old days it was a rule to rest on the day before a race. Most skiers today prefer to have an easy day on Race Day minus 2, and then some fairly light interval training on gentle uphills on Race Day minus 1.

On the day after the race some light skiing is preferred to complete rest. It could well be a fairly long workout, but it should be limbering up and technical skiing (skiing for fun).

Travelling should not be considered rest.

You are still waiting for that final word: "How to get there?" I am afraid there is no set answer. It is my belief that a coach may do much harm by being too dogmatic.

To be of some help to serious skiers of a fairly high caliber, I will, however, outline a year-round training program, month by month, also giving examples of a weekly schedule. It would be a fatal mistake for novice skiers or skiers with a slight training background to follow these monthly training schedules.

The program is intended for senior men. For junior men, 18 and 19 years old, I have suggested how the program might be modified or scaled down. Juniors, 16 and 17 years, and ladies, would be safe to work on a ¾ basis (i.e., scaling the program down to ¾ the training load).

But first some definitions to explain the methods of training suggested in this program:

By *distance training*, we mean continuous work (walking, running, ski-striding, skiing) of long duration (one to three hours) at a relatively moderate pace. The purpose is to accustom your body to hard work over long periods of time.

In the beginning one should jog, walk, run and ski-stride in gentle terrain at an even, moderate pace. As condition improves the tempo can be increased, until an even speed can be maintained for a considerable time. On long workouts the speed must be more moderate than on shorter workouts. As winter approaches select rougher and more varied terrain. Check your pulse. For distance training your heart rate may vary between 30-60 beats under your maximum. This means that you should not push so hard uphill that you gasp for breath (you should be able to speak normally). You should not feel stiff in the legs and back.

By *interval training*, we mean work (running, ski-striding, skiing) in a series of relatively intense sprints of varying length, separated by rest periods. Interval training can be divided into three categories:

1) *Short* sprints of 15 up to 60 seconds, the length of the rest periods not to exceed the duration of the sprint. (This kind of interval training is not used very much by top skiers on dry land, but may be introduced as natural interval on snow—see No. 3 below.

2) *Long* sprints of 3 up to 10 minutes, rest periods as in No. 1 above. (This kind of interval training is used more often by top skiers.)

3) *Natural* interval training takes place on a training trail where the variation in the terrain creates an interval effect. Sprints of varying length and hills of varying steepness. (This is the kind of interval training used most often by top cross-country skiers.)

For all kinds of interval training, your heart rate at the end of a sprint should be 10-15 beats under your maximum, and for natural interval even 15-20 beats under, as this kind of interval training usually is of longer duration.

After each uphill you should be on the point of feeling stiff and gasping for breath. But interval training, as the term is used in this program, is not a maximum effort. It is aerobic work.

By *tempo training* we mean work (running, ski-striding, skiing) in a series of sprints so intense that you incur oxygen debt—i.e., your working muscles (especially your legs) feel stiff. This is anaerobic work.

The purpose of tempo training is to enable your body to maintain the speed required in a race. The activity periods can last from one minute up to 20 minutes, and should not be repeated more than four or five times in one workout. Rest periods should be long enough so that you feel rested. Tempo training should not be exaggerated. Most top cross-country racers do not start it until November.

METHODS OF MOVEMENT

Movements cannot be properly described on paper; they must be shown in the field. I shall, however, try to describe briefly what is meant in this program by "walking," "running," and "ski-striding."

Walking— A brisk walk to emphasize skiing movements such as the kick. Feet should point directly forward and the kicking leg should be completely extended. Body should be in a relaxed position and arms swinging naturally forward and back.

Running—Much like a normal run, but with a more "swaying" stride and with relatively long steps aided by strong and rapid kicks. Point the feet forward and keep the body relaxed.

Ski-striding—A brisk stride in imitation of diagonal skiing. Steps are longer and forward knee more bent than in ordinary walking. Start your kick on a flat foot and bring leg to full extension. Keep the body relaxed and arms swinging naturally. Can be done in many variations ("bounce step" etc.). With poles, the ski-stride is an actual copy of the uphill stride on skis.

YEAR-ROUND TRAINING SURVEY

Hours	MAY	JUNE	JULY	AUGUST	SEPTEMBER	OCTOBER	NOVEMBER	DECEMBER	JANUARY	FEBRUARY	MARCH	APRIL

Races (2-4) — December/January

Races (8-12) — January

Races (about 10) — February

Races — March

Distance training

Interval training

Roller skiing (rowing)
(Physiologically, roller skiing is mainly distance training.)

Pulleys (strength)

Tempo training

MAY

WAY OF TRAINING	HOURS OF TRAINING		DAYS OF TRAINING	
	PER WEEK	PER MONTH	PER WEEK	PER MONTH
Distance	2½	10		
Interval	1	4		
Tempo	0	0		
Roller skiing*	1	4		
Pulleys/strength	½	2		
TOTAL	5	20	3	12

Example of weekly program:

First day:		Distance training— walk, ski stride, run in easy terrain.	1½ hr.
Second day:	1)	Light interval training— walk, ski-stride, run in varied terrain.	1 hr.
	2)	Roller skiing*—	1 hr.
Third day:	1)	Distance training— same as on first day but in slightly varied terrain.	1 hr.
	2)	Pulleys— exercises for back, abdomen, leg muscles.	½ hr.
		Total:	5 hours

*If no roller skis available, exercise arm, back, abdomen, leg muscles. Rowing is fine.

JUNE

WAY OF TRAINING	HOURS OF TRAINING		DAYS OF TRAINING	
	PER WEEK	PER MONTH	PER WEEK	PER MONTH
Distance	3½	14		
Interval	1	4		
Tempo	0	0		
Roller skiing*	2	8		
Pulleys/strength	½	2		
TOTAL	7	28	4	16

Example of weekly program:

First day:		Distance training— walk, ski-stride, run in easy terrain.	2½ hr.
Second day:	1)	Interval training (natural interval)— walk, ski-stride, run in varied terrain.	1 hr.
	2)	Roller skiing*— double poling, double-pole stride.	1 hr.

Third day:	1)	Distance training— walk, ski-stride, run in slightly varied terrain.	1 hr.
	2)	Roller skiing*— double poling, double-pole stride.	1 hr.
Fourth day:		Pulleys— exercises for back, abdomen, leg muscles.	½ hr. Total: 7 hr.

If no roller skis available, exercise arm, back, abdomen, leg muscles. Rowing is fine.

JULY

WAY OF TRAINING	HOURS OF TRAINING		DAYS OF TRAINING	
	PER WEEK	PER MONTH	PER WEEK	PER MONTH
Distance	3½	14		
Interval	2½	10		
Tempo	0	0		
Roller skiing*	1¾	7		
Pulleys/strength	½	2		
TOTAL	8¼	33	4	16

Example of weekly program:

First day:		Distance training— walk, ski-stride, run in rolling terrain.	2½ hr.
Second day:	1)	Interval training— natural intervals in varied terrain.	1½ hr.
	2)	Roller skiing*—	¾ hr.
Third day:	1)	Distance training (in rolling terrain)	1 hr.
	2)	Roller skiing*—	1 hr.
Fourth day:	1)	Interval training (light, long intervals)	1 hr.
	2)	Pulleys— strength exercises.	½ hr.
		Total:	8¼ hr.

(Fourth day's interval training to be left out by juniors.)

If no roller skis available, exercise arm, back, abdomen, leg muscles.

AUGUST

WAY OF TRAINING	HOURS OF TRAINING		DAYS OF TRAINING	
	PER WEEK	PER MONTH	PER WEEK	PER MONTH
Distance	4½	18		
Interval	3¼	13		
Tempo	0	0		
Roller skiing*	2¾	11		
Pulleys/strength	¾	3		
TOTAL	11¼	45	6	24

Example of weekly program:

First day:		Distance training—rolling terrain.	2½ hr.

First day: Distance training—   2½ hr.
                          rolling terrain.

Second day: 1)   Interval training—   1 hr.
                     natural intervals in varied terrain.
               2)   Roller skiing*—   ¾ hr.

Third day: 1)   Distance training   2 hr.
               2)   Pulleys—   ½ hr.
                     strength exercises.

Fourth day: 1)   Interval training—   1¼ hr.
                     long intervals in hilly terrain.
               2)   Roller skiing*—   ½ hr.

Fifth day: 1)   Interval training—   1 hr.
                     light, natural intervals in varied terrain.
               2)   Pulleys—   ¼ hr.

Sixth day: Roller skiing*—   1½ hr.

                                                          Total: 11¼ hr.

(Juniors to omit fourth day. The other days could also be somewhat modified.)

*If no roller skis available, exercise arm, back, abdomen, leg muscles. Ski-striding
(walking) with poles may also be introduced instead of roller skiing.*

SEPTEMBER

WAY OF TRAINING	HOURS OF TRAINING		DAYS OF TRAINING	
	PER WEEK	PER MONTH	PER WEEK	PER MONTH
Distance	6¼	25		
Interval	3½	14		
Tempo	0	0		
Roller skiing*	3	12		
Pulleys/strength	¼	1		
TOTAL	13	52	6	24

Example of weekly program:

First day: Distance training—   3 hr.

Second day: 1)   Interval training (natural)   1 hr.
               2)   Roller Skiing*   1 hr.

Third day: 1)   Distance training   2 hr.
               2)   Pulleys   ¼ hr.

Fourth day: 1)   Interval training—   1 hr.
                     long intervals in hilly terrain.
               2)   Roller skiing*   1 hr.

Fifth day:	1)	Distance training	1¼ hr.
	2)	Interval training—	¼ hr.
		ski-striding (walking) with poles.	
Sixth day:	1)	Interval training—	1¼ hr.
		natural intervals	
	2)	Roller skiing*	1 hr.

Total: 13 hr.

(Juniors to reduce first day by 50% and omit interval training on sixth day.)

If no roller skis available, exercise arm, back, abdomen, leg muscles.

OCTOBER

WAY OF TRAINING	HOURS OF TRAINING		DAYS OF TRAINING	
	PER WEEK	PER MONTH	PER WEEK	PER MONTH
Distance	6	24,		
Interval	4	16		
Tempo	0	0		
Roller skiing*	3	12		
Pulleys/strength	½	2		
TOTAL	13½	54	6	24

Example of weekly program:

First day:		Distance training—	3 hr.
		hilly terrain, steady pace uphill, check pulse.	
Second day:	1)	Interval training (natural)	1¼ hr.
	2)	Roller skiing*	1¼ hr.
Third day:	1)	Distance training—	1½ hr.
		hilly terrain, steady pace, check pulse.	
	2)	Roller skiing*	1 hr.
Fourth day:		Interval training—	1½ hr.
		for the last two weeks: harder pace uphill approaching oxygen debt (can be done with poles).	
Fifth day:	1)	Distance training—	1½ hr.
		hilly terrain, approaching interval effect.	
	2)	Ski-striding (walking)—	½ hr.
		with poles. Strength exercises.	
Sixth day:	1)	Interval training (long)—	1¼ hr.
		maintain speed uphill.	
	2)	Roller skiing*	¾ hr.

Total: 13½ hr.

(Juniors to omit third day. The other days could also be somewhat modified.)

If no roller skis available, exercise arm, back, abdomen, leg muscles.

NOVEMBER
(and onwards until snow comes)

WAY OF TRAINING	HOURS OF TRAINING		DAYS OF TRAINING	
	PER WEEK	PER MONTH	PER WEEK	PER MONTH
Distance	6¼	25		
Interval	3½	14		
Tempo	½	2		
Roller skiing*	3	12		
Pulleys/strength	¼	1		
TOTAL	13½	54	6	24

Example of weekly program:

First day:		Distance training— hilly terrain, steady pace uphill.	3 hr.
Second day:	1)	Interval training (natural)	1½ hr.
	2)	Roller skiing*	1 hr.
Third day:	1)	Distance training— hilly terrain, steady pace.	1¾ hr.
	2)	Roller skiing*	1 hr.
Fourth day:		Interval training— long intervals in hilly terrain, also some ski- striding and running with poles.	1½ hr.
Fifth day:	1)	Distance training— hilly terrain, approaching interval effect.	1½ hr.
	2)	Roller skiing*	1 hr.
Sixth day:	1)	Interval training— approaching oxygen debt. Also some oxygen debt training with poles.	1 hr.
	2)	Pulleys	¼ hr.

Total: 13½ hr.

(Juniors to omit third day. The other days can also be somewhat modified.)

If no roller skis available, exercise arm, back, abdomen, leg muscles.

You will notice that for September, October and November there has been little or no increase in the number of hours of training. But *intensity* has increased. As already mentioned, November is the heaviest month for top international skiers—on snow all the time, two workouts per day.

TRANSITION PERIOD FROM DRY-LAND TO ON-SNOW TRAINING

This period is extremely important for success later in the season. The difference between dry-land and on-snow training is great and the transition should be made with care. For the first weeks of this period it is advisable to do some training on foot (light interval training).

The first workouts on skis should concentrate on style and technique on a good, firm track in gentle terrain in order to get used to the movements and rhythm of skiing.

If you feel that you cannot get your balance right, or that your kick is not effective, you may do some skiing without poles.

For obvious reasons, the training program for this period cannot be fixed in time and duration. It depends on when and how much snow comes. One general rule is: ski as much as possible in this period.

Here is an example of a weekly program for this period, which should last for at least two weeks:

First day:		Distance training on skis— Good, firm tracks, gentle terrain. Ski with an easy gliding rhythm.	2 hr.
Second day:		Distance training on skis— same as on the first day.	1½ hr.
Third day:	1)	Distance training on skis.	1¼ hr.
	2)	Light interval training on foot.	¾ hr.
Fourth day:		Distance training on skis.	3 hr.
Fifth day:	1)	Distance training on skis.	1¼ hr.
	2)	Light interval training on foot.	¾ hr.
Sixth day:		Distance training on skis.	2½ hr.

Total: 13 hr.

Training should increase in intensity when you have become "broken in," and parts of the training should be on a more demanding trail—an *interval loop*.

The interval loop should be set in varied, hilly terrain, with short and long, gentle and steep hills varying in length from 10 to 150 meters and coming in fairly close succession after each other. Such a loop provides technique training and natural interval training.

For the practical purpose of maintaining a good track, the interval loop need not be longer than two to three kilometers. If an interval loop is not available, a single hill can be used.

Remember that going fast on skis means a high speed *forward*. It does not mean rapid arm and leg movements. Keep a relaxed body, maintain as great a forward speed as possible without losing style. Skis are made to *glide* on.

Provided that you have had at least two weeks of easy, long skiing in the latter half of November-beginning of December, a weekly program for your further training on snow may be something like this:

DECEMBER

WAY OF TRAINING	HOURS OF TRAINING		DAYS OF TRAINING	
	PER WEEK	PER MONTH	PER WEEK	PER MONTH
Distance	5½	22		
Interval	4¾	19		
Tempo	1	4		
Roller skiing	0	0		
Pulleys/strength	0	0		
TOTAL	11¾	45	6	24

Example of weekly program:

First day: Interval training (natural)—   1½ hr.
                  firm track, varied terrain, check pulse.

Second day: Distance training   3 hr.

Third day: Interval training (natural)   1¾ hr.

Fourth day: Tempo interval training—   1 hr.
                  four series of 10-15 min.

Fifth day: Distance training—   2½ hr.
                  easy terrain.

Sixth day: Interval training (natural)—   1½ hr.
                  same as on first day.

                                              Total: 11¼ hr.

(Juniors should modify the program by cutting down on second and fifth days. Races are classified as tempo training. Do not overdo them in this period—two to four should be sufficient.)

JANUARY

WAY OF TRAINING	HOURS OF TRAINING		DAYS OF TRAINING	
	PER WEEK	PER MONTH	PER WEEK	PER MONTH
Distance	4¼	17		
Interval	2½	10		
Tempo	2¼	9		
Roller skiing	0	0		
Pulleys/strength	0	0		
TOTAL	9	36	6	24

Example of weekly program:

First day: Race   1 hr.

Second day: Light interval training—   1½ hr.
                  varied terrain, feel the joy of skiing.

Third day: Distance training—   2½ hr.
                  varied but not too steep terrain, some skiing in
                  loose snow (three to five inches deep).

Fourth day:	Tempo (oxygen debt) training— firm track in varied terrain, relaxed movements between the tempo sprints; or Race (about 1 hour).	1¼ hr.
Fifth day:	Distance training	1¾ hr.
Sixth day:	Light interval training— interval loop.	1 hr.
	Total:	9 hr.

(Juniors to cut down the training for the third day.)

FEBRUARY–MARCH

Training during these months generally follows the program for January. However, it is more important than for any other period that training should be adjusted to suit the number of races, the personal needs and the desires of the individual skier.

Races should be classified as tempo training. If you race often (two to three times a week) you should cut out your tempo training altogether and concentrate on distance and lighter interval training. Even if you're travelling and racing often, you should try to get in at least one long distance workout per week, to preserve your strength and stamina. In addition, do some light natural interval training where you ski for fun and build up your "spark."

If competitive will and spark are lacking, it is advisable to avoid competition.

In races a skier will often detect his deficiencies. A speedy but " weak" skier should concentrate on more distance training, whereas a slow skier with good endurance should concentrate more on interval and tempo training.

APRIL

It is impossible to set down any definite training program for April, due to variable conditions of snow throughout the country. Winter and spring blend into one another and for most skiers April is another period of transition and adjustment to dry-land.

A fixed program may not be desirable in any event. Let April and May, to some extent, be months when you do not think seriously about training and racing. Enjoy the spring season. But it would not be advisable to let your conditioning deteriorate altogether, either.

If you have snow, ski as much as you can. Go on long tours at a moderate speed. Ski mainly for fun, but give some thought to technique and style. You can take your time now!

If you have no snow, do some easy jogging a couple of times a week, without tying yourself down to a set program.

As you then get more and more adjusted to dry-land training, you will be ready to start in at the beginning of the program we have outlined.

This year-round training program is based on Norwegian experience. I may add that our methods are primarily built on the experience of generations of competitive skiers, and to a small extent on theory and research. Whether this empiricism will be good enough for the future, I am not willing to predict. (As you know, predictions are always difficult.) What success we have had so far is above all the result of a *natural* approach. There is nothing finicky or artsy-craftsy about Norwegian cross-country training methods.

Our top skiers do more training than indicated by the program outlined here. What I have suggested should be regarded as a norm to be adapted to personal and local circumstances.

5
Skiers
Of All Ages

In nordic skiing, international competitors tend to get most of the attention. But four groups of skiers who make up an important part of the nordic racing scene are junior (high school) skiers, collegiate racers, senior (over 40) skiers and citizen racers. This chapter focuses on training ideas and programs for these four groups.

In the opening article, former international racer turned junior coach Peter Davis presents his approach to coaching young skiers at the Lyndon Nordic Training Center in Vermont. It's a detailed article, by a capable coach who never loses sight of the fact that the junior skier is, above all, young.

Age isn't a factor with the collegiate skier, who generally is old enough to take on a full-scale adult training program. But time definitely is a factor, since the collegian must combine training and studying. "This presents the problem of how to train for strength and endurance in a limited amount of time," says University of Colorado coach Kim Kendall in his article, "Skiing at C.U." In the article, Kendall describes the year-round nordic training program of the championship Colorado team, and offers valuable technique advice as well as some highly interesting information on how physiological and psychological testing is used to help skiers on his team.

Time available for training rather than age is also the main limiting factor for senior (over 40) skiers. At least that's the view expressed by the '74 US senior champion Einar Svensson in his article "The Senior (Over 40) Skier." "From my experience," he says, "there is no substantial difference in training based on age, except in time available and spent on training. The older person, fully employed, usually does not have the freedom to train as often and as long as the younger person who sometimes can devote 100% of his time to skiing."

The 48-year-old, Scandinavian-born Svensson, a Seattle engineer by profession, offers the over-40 skier advice on how to get started in training and how to organize a year-round program. Included in the article is a complete description of his own training.

The concluding article in this chapter is by former US national coach Sven Wiik, who offers training advice to the average citizen racer.

TRAINING JUNIORS

by Peter Davis

Peter Davis was a six-year veteran of the US Ski Team when he accepted a full-time position in '73 as director of the Lyndon Nordic Training Center at Lyndon Institute, Lyndon Center, Vermont. The Lyndon Institute is a high school of some 550 students (50 of whom are boarding students), and the program that the tall (6' 6"), personable Davis directs is probably unique in the US— —a nine-month-a-year cross-country ski training/tutorial program which offers young skiers a chance to continue their education while engaged in a full-time training and racing program. In '74 half of the skiers in the program qualified for the US Junior Nationals; one of the girls competed in the Women's Senior Nationals, finishing fifth in the five-kilometer. As the program becomes more widely known, Davis hopes to attract promising young skiers from all over the US to come to Lyndon to live, study and train.

Author's Note: The United States Ski Association classifies a junior as any skier, male or female, under the age of 18 years, nine months, as of Dec. 31 of each ski season. This method of classification seems designed to harmonize more with the American high school athletic system than with the international classification standards. A European junior is any female under 19 and any male under 20, as of Dec. 31. Recently, there has been an effort on the part of the United States Ski Association to more closely equate American juniors with international juniors by creating "junior men's" and "junior women's" classes following the international standard. But in this discussion, however, the word "junior" refers to American juniors, i.e., skiers under 18 years, nine months.

For most of my years as an active competitor, I was self-coached and depended on my imagination, perception and a critical eye to formulate my own training program. Since my retirement from the United States Ski team in 1973, I have been working with junior skiers, both girls and boys, at the Lyndon Nordic Training Center. Coming directly from the national program as I did, I was able to draw a great deal from my experiences at that level, but that in itself was not the best preparation for coaching, especially coaching juniors. I found myself reaching further back to the days when the only coach I had was me and the only thing that kep my motivation high through the thousands of solo training hours was imagination, being able to incorporate variety into a training program.

WORKING EFFECTIVELY WITH JUNIORS

You need imagination to work effectively with junior skiers, and I try to use as much imagination as possible in planning our training here. I try to avoid duplicating a workout in the same month, for instance. I change the starting point of a workout regularly, change the scenery daily, and try to interject a new "twist" or idea into every workout. Done right, you will have a varied, imaginative training program that will repay itself in very significant dividends.

Cross-country skiing is a very technically and physically demanding sport. Consequently, it requires long hours of training. When working with junior cross-country skiers, you must always remember that their training at this level is, mainly, preparation for later years of skiing. Therefore, it's important that the training stimulates their interest and keeps it at a high level. An imaginatively-constructed training program will do that. But more than that, such a program will actually permit the skier to handle a heavier training load since he'll tend to be more physically eager and mentally alert with a variety of training.

It wasn't long ago that the best skiers in the US were beginning to adopt the idea of specific ski training in the off-season. Now it is the acceptable way to train for cross-country skiing even at the junior level; the more movements you can do in your training that are ski-related, the more natural and technically proficient a skier you will become. I believe strongly in this concept.

Therefore, at the Lyndon Nordic Training Center, we stress that our skiers think like skiers during the full year and especially during all our dry-land training. On foot runs we simulate a partial ski motion (called a ski bounce) on uphills and on extended hikes we "ski walk." We pull arm resistance devices that simulate the poling motion; we hill bound with poles and we place special emphasis on roller skiing, especially with the kick, double-pole motion. Seldom do we train without incorporating some aspect of ski-related motion and technique.

I have heard some junior coaches say, "Oh, don't worry about your technique until you get on snow." However, I feel that the more time the junior skier spends on ski motions before the season, the further ahead he will be when he gets on snow. For example, we've had skiers who were so technically inefficient when they began training with us in the fall that it was pathetic. But by stressing ski motions in the dry-land program, I have seen a 300 percent technical improvement in some of them before the first snowflake falls!

THE COACH'S GREATEST DUTY

The greatest duty of the junior coach is to give his young skiers all the technical skills he can, because the style and habits a person formulates in a matter of months as a junior may stay with him through his career. The attention the junior coach and his athletes pay to technique now can later be shifted to developing the cardiovascular system.

Obviously, a good junior coach must be a good technical critic and must be able to translate technique problems to his skiers effectively. If the coach feels inadequate in this area, he should spend time studying movies of accomplished skiers, analyzing and picking up the fine points of good technique.

I often feel that if a junior cross-country coach were to have only one attribute, it should be a good critical eye for technique. Then at least his skiers would be assured of the technical corrections and refinements that are so imperative for competitive success in later years.

Again, a coach needs imagination, as well as perception, to develop a good variety of ski-related workouts. The real key here is to analyze the sport, the muscles involved, the dynamics and physics that come into play, and what has to

"We stress that our skiers think like skiers during the full year and especially during all our dry-land training."

be accomplished. Since cross-country skiing is so technical, much more than, say, cross-country footrunning, there are more areas of emphasis, more areas to study and condition. A good coach will be able to devise a number of ski-related workouts just by picking out individual technical problems or weaknesses of his skiers.

Beyond technical efficiency, juniors need work in technical strength (i.e., specific strength for skiing). In recent years I have seen the lead in this sport pass from the smooth technicians to the somewhat less smooth, but very strong, powerful skiers. I don't think juniors are too young to work on strength; so we have a number of workouts specifically designed (or suited) to develop arm and leg strength and power. Weight lifting, hiking with packs, carrying another person piggyback for a short distance, are all good strength workouts. And an exercise called "harness pulling" which we originated has many applications.

We simply take some old bicycle inner tubes, cut two of them in half and tie them together. Then a skier, with the inner tube around the waist, ski bounds or ski walks up an incline while a partner of about the same height and weight restrains him. The body position of the skier in the exercise closely duplicates the body position in actual skiing.

The exercise came about simply from analyzing the technical demands of the sport and using some imagination to apply them to training. We have found many useful ways of using this exercise with our juniors at Lyndon, and leg and arm power have improved as a result.

ENDURANCE, SPEED AND STRESS

As you've noticed, thus far I have not talked about the real "meat" of training junior skiers—distance running and skiing. That's because I wanted to expose you first to some very basic ground rules of coaching young skiers, to set the theoretical tone, if you will. As far as conditioning is concerned, even juniors must prepare several months in advance for their season. High-school-aged skiers should be involved in a minimum six-month program—four months of conditioning for two months of racing. Most of the skiers at the Lyndon Nordic Training Center are involved in a 12-month program—nine months of ski-type training for three months of racing.

Fully 80 percent of a junior's conditioning program must be focused around endurance-type foot running, roller skiing, or snow skiing. Since cross-country skiing is an endurance sport, the development of an efficient cardiovascular system is both implied and essential. Again, it is important to have variety in the program and mileage should be accumulated only under progressive and stimulating conditions.

Quality or speed-type training is included in a junior program along with endurance training but it increases in amount as the ski season approaches and then during the season itself. Interval, natural interval, and fartlek are the best quality training methods since they duplicate the same type of interval that one encounters during a ski race in climbing hills.

Talking about quality and interval training brings to mind another important concept in working with junior skiers—stress. It is difficult to talk in concrete terms about stress, although any coach who has worked to any extent at all with runners or skiers can tell you he has seen it. In planning a training program for junior cross-country skiers, careful consideration should be given to the training load and the individual's ability to handle it.

I believe that any sound training program must be structured around periods of rest and stress. This is especially important with younger athletes. The difficult part is determining *how much* rest and stress. So many coaches place priority on mileage trained, or total hours trained, and forget to read the sign posts of fatigue and stress along the way.

One simple stress guide I use is the individual resting pulse. I encourage my skiers to record their resting pulse each morning, to help them understand how their body is reacting over a period of time to different types of workouts, and to enable them to detect fatigue and stress (the tell-tale sign would be a significant rise in the resting heart rate).

Junior cross-country skiers must be trained progressively and logically from year to year. That is not to say that stress or quality isn't good; in fact, it is absolutely essential in order to broaden physical limits. But the training program must allow for rebuilding and physical adaptation.

At Lyndon, most of our juniors respond well to a very structured training program that follows a weekly cycle: two days of training, a day of rest, three days of training, another day of rest. We make exceptions both ways for skiers with shallow and deep training bases. Generally, however, I have found this to be a most successful pattern in dealing with fatigue and allowing for a steady, progressive development of a wide group of junior skiers.

Illness and injury are sometimes stress in disguise. A perceptive junior coach can interpret these signs and adjust the individual's training program. There are no illnesses that are particularly indigenous to cross-country skiers, unless it might be the common cold and bronchitis. The sinus membranes are more active during cold weather and if a skier is slightly fatigued, he is most apt to catch some sort of a cold.

I generally interpret any cold as a sign of lower resistance and low stress, and so I heed the sign. It's particularly important to avoid competition during the period before a cold has peaked, since the cold weather can irritate the bronchial tubes and sometimes trigger a transfer of the cold to the chest.

Injuries in cross-country skiing are far less common than in almost any other sport. And if it were possible to ski the year round, I daresay there would be no injuries in cross-country skiing at all—short of falling on the course and somehow contracting an impact injury. The injuries usually encountered, such as tendonitis, chondromalchia, stress fractures, etc., are generally a result of dry-land training programs and often carry over to the winter months.

In coaching juniors, I see shin splints and knee injuries often during the fall program. These are better prevented than cured and it is relatively easy to follow the guidelines we follow at the Lyndon Nordic Training Center: avoid any running on tarred or asphalt surfaces; dirt roads and woods provide softer footing and generally offer variable terrain more suited to the needs of the cross-country skier. Any person with a limited amount of training background is susceptible to stress or over-use injuries in the fall; such a person should be encouraged to do the running workouts on "soft" ground.

AN ABILITY TO SEE THINGS AS A GAME

To this point I have directed a lot of information and ideas at you, and perhaps all of it hasn't come to a focus in your mind yet. One final point should help. It was at first difficult for me to grasp the fact when I began working with juniors, that life for them still hasn't taken on that cold, serious appearance of reality. The wonderful thing about youngsters is that they are able, in their magical minds, to regard most things as some sort of a game. They regard cross-country ski training no differently.

Every attempt should be made to make training for juniors fun. Games like soccer or relays always lighten up the seriousness of training, but even more difficult individual workouts can take on a fun appearance simply in the way they are designed and administered by the coach. Again, our friend imagination crops up; it takes imagination to make the many hours of training fun. As I mentioned earlier, training for juniors is primarily preparation for later years of skiing; if that training isn't made enjoyable, the junior's involvement with the sport is destined to be cut short. The junior coach, therefore, has a heavy responsibility.

One coaching technique that I feel is most helpful in working effectively with young cross-country skiers is to actually train with your athletes. By doing this, you get the fullest opportunity to use your imagination, perception and technical knowledge. When you train with your athletes, you can redesign the workout after it has started, if you find, for instance, that the workout is more than the group can handle on a particular day, or you want to have some individual skiers do more or less. If the group mood is too serious or too light, you can try to influence it in the right direction. Of course, the more you're with the athletes, the more technical assistance you're able to offer—and there's no better time to offer such assistance than during the actual training session.

Probably the best reason to train with your young skiers is so that you are able to feel the level of stress and fatigue that they are undergoing. The wisest coach in the world can sit at a desk and say a workout should consist of this and that, but unless he is out there, running all the hills, doing all the skiing, he has no real sense of what he is asking the athlete to do.

There are so many variables to coaching cross-country skiing and high school athletes that an effective coach cannot afford *not* to be around his skiers while they are training. Plus there is a special relationship that develops between coach and athlete when they train together, and that relationship cannot be developed in any other way.

Perhaps in no other sport are the skills of a coach tested so fully and thoroughly as in junior cross-country skiing. The coach must be innovative, critical and perceptive to interpret problems, design stimulating workouts, provide technical guidance, and sense the moods, attitudes and thoughts of his skiers. It's a big job. But I think a coach who applies some of the concepts and methods that I have outlined here will find a healthy, happy and productive group of skiers under his watch.

At the Lyndon Nordic Training Center, we are lucky to have a unique and compatible environment for cross-country ski training. Training for these skiers takes on a flavor of fun, and they actually learn to develop a training lifestyle, where cross-country skiing is a positive, and essential part of their lives. And that, I feel, is what training must be to them—enjoyable and natural—if they're to cope with the long-range requirements and achieve competitive success in a totally demanding sport like cross-country skiing.

SKIING AT C.U.

by Kim Kendall

The University of Colorado in Boulder, Colo. has dominated US intercollegiate skiing the past three years, winning three National Collegiate Athletic Association championships in succession. Twenty-three-year-old Kim Kendall is CU's cross-country ski coach under the school's head ski coach Bill Marolt. Kim came to the University of Colorado in '73 after graduating from the University of New Hampshire. He is a fine ski competitor himself. In '72 and '73 he was the NCAA Skimeister (title given to the best all-round skier—downhill, cross-country, jumping and nordic combined—at the NCAA Championships). Kim was fourth in the nordic combined in the '73 US National Championships.

It is difficult to say when a cross-country competitor starts and ends a season. For many of the more serious skiers it never ends. And, of course, the continual build-up of years of training adds immeasurably to an individual's strength and endurance.

For the world's best cross-country racers, training is a full-time job. For the college competitor, it's somewhat different. The collegian must budget his time between studying and training if he's to do both effectively. This presents the problem of how to train for strength and endurance in a limited amount of time. Many coaches use different methods of training and I don't pretend that my method is the best, but it has been successful on the college racing circuit.

We start training the first week of school and practice five times a week. With the National Collegiate Athletic Association Championships held in March, that leaves the coaches six months to train their skiers. (During the summer months the skiers are expected to maintain a light physical training program consisting of long-distance running, roller skiing and weight training.)

Each of our practice sessions in the fall begin with a short run to loosen up, followed by 10-15 minutes of calisthenics. We stretch all the muscles, paying particular attention to those muscles that will be under the greatest stress during the actual workout. If the workout is to be a long run, we protect against cramps in the calf muscles by stretching the achilles tendons and lower leg flexors, the gastrocnemius and soleus. If the workout includes sprints, the quadriceps and hamstrings must be stretched and warmed up to prevent pulled muscles.

After warming up, we start the workout proper. A typical week of dry-land training consists of the following workouts:

Tuesday—long flat run lasting 75-90 minutes, followed by 20-30 minutes weight training.

Wednesday—10-12 mile hike in the mountains (maximum elevation rise: 2500 feet).

Thursday—60 minutes roller skiing, followed by 20-30 minutes weight training.

Friday—12-18 mile run (elevation rise: 2000 feet).

Saturday—60 minutes roller skiing.

(Sunday and Monday are days that most of the skiers use to catch up on their studies.)

The hikes vary in distance and type of terrain to avoid boredom and repetition. I feel that a training program consisting of running only is not thorough enough to properly condition a cross-country ski racer. Skiing utilizes and involves many more muscles than does running. To develop all of these muscles we roller ski and lift weights. Both are excellent upper body builders that develop strength and endurance.

Cross-country skiing requires snow but unfortunately snow is not always available; so you have to substitute roller skiing for skiing in training. Roller skiing is as close an activity to cross-country skiing as is practical and possible. It involves many of the same muscle groups skiing does, as well as the same kick-and-glide motion.

We roller ski on roads that are not heavily travelled and vary in terrain as do cross-country courses. Sixty minutes of roller skiing not only gives the arms a work-

Skiing behind someone else is an excellent way to improve your stride and learn to "read the terrain." (Robert George photo)

out but develops the respiratory system and lower back muscles. The back muscles are often neglected by many cross-country skiers. The result can be cramped muscles, causing lost seconds in a race. If roller skiing cannot be included in the dry-land training program, two exercises can be done to strengthen the back:

A) back raises done lying face down on the floor, hands behind the neck, and lifting the upper body;

B) holding a light weight behind the head while standing, lower the trunk until parallel to the floor, then return to an upright standing position (use a 40-50 pound weight and do three sets of 15).

Although physical training is the primary factor for successful cross-country racing, it is not the only means available to obtain a desired end. The University of Colorado is fortunate in that it has one of the most complete physiology testing laboratories in the country. We test muscle strength of arms and legs, percent body fat and reaction time. Most important, though, is the oxygen uptake test of the cardiovascular system. In this test, the skier runs on a treadmill and the air he breathes out is collected in large bags. The air is then analyzed for carbon dioxide and the amount of oxygen extracted from the air. The oxygen extracted and burned is the key to efficient body function during exercise. The oxygen uptake test, therefore, is the most valid means of measuring an individual's ability to utilize oxygen for work output. Through this test and the strength test, it's possible to isolate a muscle weakness so specific exercises can be done to overcome the weakness. For example, a test shows that the left leg is much weaker than the right. Specific weight training, such as a 30-minute daily workout with a weighted shoe or on a weight machine can be used to strengthen the weaker leg.

In any competitive sport, the individual's psychological attitude toward competition is a significant, often crucial factor. This is overlooked by many coaches. I feel that the athlete's mental attitude is a major influence on his level of performance over a series of races and in a given race. And it should be the job of every

CAMROSE LUTHERAN COLLEGE
Library

coach to know under what psychological conditions and at what emotional level each athlete performs best.

In order for head coach Bill Marolt and myself to obtain this information, we have the competitors fill out a psychological report each year. This report includes past athletic performances, future goals in competition, assessment of factors interfering with performance, and conditions when optimal performance occurred. After completing this report, the team meets with a psychologist for lessons in relaxation and mental imagery. Mental imagery is the conscious effort to fantasize perfect technique and its execution. In other words, it's concentrated daydreaming of skiing cross-country perfectly.

Each team member then meets individually with the psychologist to discuss his emotional level during competition and the problems it may cause. What we are looking for is enough feedback so each skier knows under what conditions he performs best so that he can duplicate those conditions and feelings prior to starting a race.

Although physical and psychological testing are part of the training program at the University of Colorado, skiing remains the most important preparation of all. We start skiing as early as possible, usually the first or second week in November. The first couple of days on snow we ski slow and easy to gain balance and become accustomed to movements on snow. After that, we start a program of long, slow skiing two to three hours each day to tone the muscles needed for racing. We do not point for our first races, which are in December. Instead, we use them as speed practice. The first race or two is not a valid indicator of how one will perform three months later in the NCAA Championships anyway. Therefore, to avoid reaching maximum physical condition too early in the year, we concentrate mostly on distance and technique. At the same time we maintain a foot-running program to supplement the skiing.

Since technique is one area where there's always room for improvement, our technique training is continuous. We start out on flat terrain to practice proper diagonal striding and skiing corners. We try to ski long smooth and rhythmical strides with full extension of arms and legs. In skiing corners, if the turn is gradual with a well-prepared track, then a shortening up of the inside stride and a lengthening of the outside stride will provide maximum speed through the turn. If the turn is sharp, then a quick double pole before the corner and a skate turn followed by another double pole after the corner will prove to be the most effective.

Learning to "read the terrain," to know when it is fastest to double pole or single stick, is acquired through much practice. Skiing behind another person is one of the best teaching methods for improving one's ability to read terrain.

Skiing up hills is often the weakest part of a skier's technique. Everytime we ski, a little time is spent on uphill technique. When the grade is short and steep and the herringbone is necessary, the racer must learn agility and balance for the quick weight transfer from ski to ski, bounding fashion of the herringbone. With long gradual slopes, the racer's tempo must quicken and the stride must shorten to maintain the necessary momentum to ascend the hill quickly.

Our winter training does not change noticeably until three weeks before the championship race. Interval training on skis and on foot (foot running) is started to quicken the skier's tempo. Each skier trains more as an individual now because he knows how long it takes for him to attain peak condition and how long he can maintain optimal performance. Some of the skiers are capable of interval training three times a week and maintaining peak condition for a couple weeks. Other skiers only feel capable of doing intervals once or twice a week and maintaining peak performance for only a week. It is up to the coach and the racer to know what's best.

Finally, it's the NCAA meet. Months and months of running, skiing, roller skiing and weight lifting goes into one 15-kilometer race. As well, the individual's confidence and mental preparation contributes greatly to the results. When it's all over— win or lose—you relax for a while, then start preparing for the next year

THE SENIOR (OVER 40) SKIER

by Einar Svensson

Einar Svensson is a three-time U.S. Veteran's (Over 40) cross-country skiing champion ('71, '73 and '74), and one of the country's most knowledgeable people on the sport. His experience and knowledge are reflected by the fact he hopes to write a book soon on nordic training.

Cross-country skiing is a very strenuous sport that requires strength and endurance in virtually every part of the body—arms, shoulders, back, abdomen, legs—and great aerobic and anaerobic fitness as well.

Senior skiers seriously interested in starting a cross-country program should first of all be healthy and should check with their doctors to ensure that they're physically capable of pursuing such a program. Conditioning should be built up evenly and systematically over a long period of time. Personal experience and knowledge about yourself will determine how hard you should push in training. As a general conditioning reference for building up your capacity for exercise, I suggest you read *Aerobics* by Dr. Kenneth Cooper.

Don't rush your program. After doing no cross-country racing for 10 years and only moderate amounts of touring between the ages of 30 and 40 because of business and family obligations, it took me several years before I began winning races again.

Cross-country racing is a sport in which it generally takes a long time to reach top performance. Most of the elite racers in the world today stay at the top and improve until they are 35 or older. Few sports can boast a statistic like that. Whether you want to improve as a tourer or top racer, you must be prepared to work at it for years, and enjoy it while doing so.

From my experience, there is no substantial difference in training based on age, except in time available and spent on training. The older person, fully employed, usually does not have the freedom to train as often and as long as a younger person who sometimes can devote 100 percent of his time to training.

STUDY TOP SKIERS

My training program, in general, is a cross-section of what the international elite use, except as a businessman, I can afford to spend only one-third as much time, or less, at training. Any skier today, including the senior, who wants to improve as much as possible, has to familiarize himself with what modern cross-country racing and training is all about. I use extensive literature from Scandinavia and Germany as guidelines. More and more studies and training information are being translated to and written in English for the general public. Study and utilize the methods the top skiers use to achieve their goals.

KEYS TO SUCCESSFUL TRAINING—
VARIETY AND EFFICIENCY

Since virtually every muscle in the body is used in cross-country skiing, the skier's training program should be highly diversified. A cross-country training program cannot be based on spending one hour or more daily jogging a long distance at uniform speed. Ski tourers, too, will reap more benefits from the varied program I suggest.

In North America, most serious skiers are well educated in conditioning themselves, but really lack the knowledge of correct skiing technique and how to simulate this technique during dry-land training.

Cross-country training must, in each and every respect, be based on usage of muscle and body motions similar to those correctly executed on snow. It is even more important for seniors, who have to really budget their time, that their program be extremely efficient. One must utilize the time available by training with maximum efficiency and intensity.

The program I follow is even more modified than normal, since I live in Seattle, 60 miles from the nearest snow, and must train after dark and usually in the rain. This type of situation is very psychologically demanding on one's spirit and willpower, to say the least. I try to keep my mind off the rain by focusing on executing each movement or exercise correctly. The effective training time of one or 1½ hours passes quickly.

Briefly, my year-round training program consists of:
a) An off-season dry-land program.
b) A transition period.
c) A ski season program which includes dry-land simulation training.

Summer Dry-land Training Schedule: three days weekly.

The off-season weekly dry-land program is scaled down in time and intensity, but otherwise contains very much the same type of exercises as the winter schedule.

All training is preceded by a 10-15 minute warmup, which may be jogging, active work, a sauna bath, etc. The training itself is divided into the following:

● 1/4 calisthenics, which includes special relaxation, stretching and strength exercises of the body parts and muscles used in cross-country skiing. Productive work, such as gardening, digging, carpentry, etc. is part of strength training if utilizing the right muscles.

- 1/4 roller skiing. Primarily a combination of double poling, except on short uphills where I do diagonal poling under high intensity. (I walk downhill.)
- 1/4 distance training, consisting of jogging, hiking, hunting, rowing, swimming. This is the "fun training." Foot running on hard surfaces such as asphalt and concrete can make one stiff and causes more ankle injuries than running on soft, springy ground—grass, moss, etc.
- 1/4 interval training, consisting of strenuous uphill ski-strides with poles, indoor exercise on friction bike, short uphill sprints (walking downhill), and special uphill roller skiing, using diagonal poling.

You do *not* do all of the above at each session, but combine two or three of them.

Transition Training Period (Sept.-Oct.-Nov.): five days weekly.

The program remains very much the same as for the summer, except that one should train more often and the intensity has picked up.

Ski Season Training Program (Dec.- Jan.-Feb.-March): four days weekly.

You have now built up your conditioning; relax your program slightly between races and enjoy your skiing.

Snow skiing replaces the greatest part of the dry-land distance and interval training.

If lack of snow is a problem as it is with me, one should regularly schedule weekends—Friday evening, Saturday and Sunday—for on-snow training. Try to ski three to four hours each Saturday and Sunday, except on days when you're racing. Supplement this weekend training when possible with mid-week evening skiing. I drive to my cabin near a lighted ski area Wednesday after work, and pack my own demanding technique loop on the outskirts of the downhill slopes. More and more commercial areas are now investing in lighted cross-country tracks which are greatly needed.

During the rest of the week in a no-snow situation, calisthenics and roller-skiing should predominate.

ADVICE ON DIET

There is a good deal of literature on diet written for other sports, running in particular. Most of it is applicable to cross-country racing and touring. It is my experience, however, that a large number of senior skiers do not know what foods and drinks to stay away from before training and races as well as during general conditioning. My advice is to read up on the subject!

HIGH-ALTITUDE RACING

International rules set 5800 feet as the maximum altitude for races, and that should be followed. There is danger for senior skiers to over-estimate themselves and cause internal heart and lung injuries which may occur under "high-altitude failure" when the skier pushes himself beyond his oxygen capacity.

THE SENIOR'S REWARD

The rewards for beginning and sticking to a continuing cross-country training program are great—particularly for the senior skier. Good health in middle and older ages, great aerobic capacity which means a supremely healthy heart and lungs, boundless energy, and not least, a knowledge and awareness of yourself, your mental and physical capacities, that only an athlete experiences. The reward is more than worth the effort.

THE CITIZEN RACER

by Sven Wiik

Sven Wiik is one of the most respected nordic skiing authorities in the US. Former ski coach at Western State College in Gunnison, Colorado, he coached the US national cross-country and nordic combined teams in the 1958 world championships and the 1960 Winter Olympics. He has also served as president of the US Ski Association's ski coaches system. Sven and his wife operate the Scandinavian Lodge in Steamboat Springs, Colo.

Cross-country skiing can be divided, basically, into two activities—the competitive sport of cross-country (or nordic) racing and the purely recreational activity of ski touring. The cross-country ski competitor trains his body and mind in order to win in competition. The ski tourer enjoys the winter leisurely. Then

we have the citizen racer, the person who enjoys everything that ski touring has to offer, but at the same time is seeking the opportunity to test himself against himself, or, in a social way, to enjoy competition with others.

I would briefly like to offer some training advice to the citizen racer. My first suggestion is: do not enter a competition without any previous training. Secondly, remember that your strong point when you have done only a little physical conditioning is your technique, your tactics and, if you are a veteran skier, in the many years of experience you have behind you. Thirdly, under no circumstances would I advise that the citizen racer with a modest training background, which is the only background he needs to enjoy citizen racing, over-exert himself, and "gut it out" at the end of a race to win or finish a few positions higher.

Unlike the serious competitor, the citizen racer does not need to go through a long, systematic dry-land training program to prepare himself for competition. (Of course, there's nothing to stop him from doing this type of training if he so desires.) My suggestion to the citizen racer is simple: keep active during the summer. You do not have to start your training before the snow arrives if all you want to do is race "a little bit." It's early enough to start training when the snow comes.

Do lots of just plain skiing to start with, breaking your own trail if need be. After this period of training, start skiing in a track, paying special attention to technique, for with technique comes effortless skiing. Technique is so important that it enables skiers in second-rate condition to out-ski opponents who are in top-notch condition. This is what the citizen racer should try to capitalize on.

There are, of course, many citizen racers who are very serious about their skiing and will train in the same way as any national or international competitor. They want to develop as much strength as possible, and will go through a well-planned pre-season and in-season conditioning program for that reason. They also want to ski technically well, and will spend a lot of time on that phase of training.

These are not, however, the citizen racers I have been addressing myself to here. I have offered this advice to the tens of thousands of citizen racers who are simply out for the pure enjoyment of skiing and racing, who train a little bit and only have the time or desire to train a little bit, but would still like to go out over the weekend and enjoy competition.

6

The Canadian Way

by Bjorger Pettersen
Coach, Canadian National Team

Bjorger Pettersen is not only Canada's national coach but personally developed many of the stars on his team through his work with the TEST program in Canada's Northwest Territories. Today a strikingly high percentage of the skiers on the Canadian team come from the Northwest Territories—among them Bert Bullock, Canada's most promising young male racer (he was fourth in the '74 European Junior Championships), the Firth sisters, Sharon and Shirley, who have won numerous Canadian and North American championships between them, and Ernie Lennie, the '74 Canadian 30-kilometer champion. Coach Pettersen and his family now live in McBride, British Columbia, where he has his own nordic skiing center, the colorfully named Ranch of the Vikings.

This article is not intended to be a complete outline on how to develop a champion cross-country skier. Such a vast subject would require a text many times longer than this.

Rather my intention is to take a look at the Canadian National Ski Team Nordic Program and some of the thinking behind it during the past 10 years.

PHILOSOPHY AND APPROACH

To me, atmosphere and motivation are the key factors needed to develop a successful cross-country program. If the proper atmosphere cannot be created for athletes to appreciate the *meaning* of cross-country excellence, then it is very difficult to create the sufficient motivation. Whenever I start a new program, I first concentrate on creating such an atmosphere.

For example, when I started the TEST (Territorial-Experimental-Ski-Training) program in Canada's Northwest Territories, I first concentrated on educating the public on the importance of their people excelling in skiing. Then I went out and developed the top of my pyramid—the superior, or star, skier. The young ski stars became the heroes or heroines admired by hundreds of youngsters, and created the atmosphere and meaning for cross-country skiing in northern Canada. Needless to say, the bottom of the pyramid developed to make the complete picture.

It is obvious that the best North American skiers over the last 15 years have been pioneers with mental barriers to fight. We still suffer from these barriers to a certain degree. The barriers are the result of the fact that we lack the culture and environment which some European countries have for the sport.

We are gradually breaking these barriers down. I believe that in Canada we are raising our standard noticeably each time we get new skiers coming onto our national team. The healthy competition of new skiers fighting for positions on our team is absolutely imperative to creating the proper environment.

ROLE OF THE COACH

Is a coach a friend, advisor or dictator?

In my opinion, a coach has to be all these things. Sport psychology is mainly common sense. I claim no special gifts in training skiers other than, perhaps, the ability to observe, analyze and understand athletes. My coaching is usually a combination of gentle understanding and dynamic encouragement. This is simply my personality. The worse mistake a coach can make is to try to be something or someone he's not. I am convinced a coach who totally copies, and does not coach in his own style, to suit his personality, is doomed to fail.

THE CANADIAN TEAM PROGRAM

During my days as a racer and coach I have studied foreign cross-country training methods a great deal. However, I feel that most of our Canadian success can be attributed to what we have learned from our own practical experiences. It is important to know the successful European methods, so we can take shortcuts in our experiments. But I feel it is even more important to know which methods are going to work best in our way of life. It may be said that the Canadian program is built on research from European programs and our own experience.

Before talking about actual training, I feel it is important for us to have a clear understanding of the "ingredients" which one finds in the make-up of a superior cross-country skier. If the maximum score was 100 and the average 50, I think the super cross-country skier would rate as indicated in the following areas:

- Aerobic conditioning—100
- Anaerobic conditioning—80
- Speed—43
- Strength—50
- Technique—100
- Flexibility—48
- Psychological strength—? (see below)

In looking at the above list, it is obvious most of the concentration in training must be on endurance training and technique. Psychological strength in international competition may be almost as important. But to date we have no way of measuring this.

The human body is a wonderful mechanism. It has the ability to adapt to the changes placed upon it. So all we have to do is place the body under heavier and heavier work loads. It will adapt to this and raise its performance level. There's one big catch: the body and the mind must have sufficient time to adapt to the gradual increase in training. With this in mind, training should not be considered as straight "bull work," but an *art*. The key to a good training program is a systematic, gradual increase in training as the body adapts to the training.

I often compare building a body up through training to building a big fire. If you throw too much wood on the fire, it will smother. If you don't add any wood, the fire gradually grows smaller. If you gradually throw more and more wood on the fire, it gradually grows larger. The same may be said of building the body up with a training program.

The skier with the best training program is the one who has found the best balance for him, between intensity and duration (length or distance). Therefore, the ideal program for any skier is the program he builds for himself based on knowledge learned from the reactions of his own body to various forms of training. I greatly believe in individualism when it comes to training, and I strongly recommend to those skiers who use my program to adapt it to their own individual training needs.

I am also a great believer in training that is specific (i.e., closely related) to cross-country skiing. Physiologists have proved that by systematic training, a person may improve in a given muscle movement—push-ups, for instance—by as much as 50 times. This will only happen, however, if the training is *specific* to the particular muscle movement. For example, you don't ride a bicycle as training to do more push-ups; you do push-ups or some other exercise that's very closely related.

The other important point stemming from this is that improvement in a given muscle movement can have little, or no, carry-over effect on another muscle movement—even one that would seem to be similar. For example, a skier may increase his push-up capacity from a maximum of 25 to 400, but only receive a one to three percent increase in *effective* poling strength.

This shows us that the best training for skiing is skiing. The next best training is the type which fits nearest to the specific body movements of cross-country skiing. In my opinion, swimming, tennis, push-ups, sprint running, basketball, football, etc., do very little, if anything, to make one a faster or better cross-country skier.

I don't totally believe that running is very good training for cross-country skiing, either. Running with a high knee lift and quick step does not train the same leg muscles as those used in skiing. You must train the kick (skiing) muscles, not the running muscles. To derive the maximum benefit from running, I feel it is important to use as many imitation steps as possible, such as the sway stride, bounce stride, ski stride, etc. In the summer these steps and roller skiing will train your oxygen transport system for the right muscles.

We use three main types of training for on-snow and dry-land: distance, interval and tempo training.

DISTANCE TRAINING

Both dry-land and snow training programs start with distance training. It may be said that distance training is the backbone of all cross-country training. It's the basic way to build all the organs and muscles important for cross-country skiing, without putting too much stress on any of them.

I would describe distance training as a type of training meant to condition the body to work near maximum capacity over long periods of time. The ideal pulse rate for distance training is 40 beats per minute below one's maximum pulse. It is essential to remember to drink liquids every 30 to 45 minutes while distance training or racing. When you loose two percent of your weight sweating, you also loose 20 per cent of your performance. Mix your drinks warm, with five to 12 percent sugar.

INTERVAL TRAINING

Interval training means what it says, running and resting in intervals. In interval training you bring the heart close to maximum, rest, then repeat the process over again. I would recommend three to 10 minutes running with two to four minutes of rest or jogging in between. The pulse after each interval should be between eight and 12 beats per minute less than maximum, and the pulse should return to between 115 and 130 beats per minutes before the start of each repetition. When the pulse doesn't return to this level, then the training should cease.

Some important things I have found about interval training: the 15-15 is too short for cross-country skiers; intervals shorter than three minutes are of little value; uphill ski stride intervals with ski poles have a tendency to make you peak early. Try to do interval training on natural terrain, as this places far less stress on the body than repetition interval training on a single hill.

TEMPO TRAINING

Basically, we use two types of tempo training. The first is meant to accustom the body to speeds equal to or above racing speeds. The second is oxygen debt training which accustoms the body to exactly what the term says—oxygen debt.

Tempo training is very hard on the body. It also brings about a tremendous increase in ability. In order not to get into shape too early and not to put too much stress on the body, this training is only recommended for the later stages of a training program.

Note of precaution: Lately a great deal of research has been done on drawnout or extended interval training sessions. The results show that a large build-up of lactic acid in the blood stream over long periods of time has a very negative effect on performance. Also, the long hours of training required can cause an overdose affect which can wear on the mind and willpower.

For tempo training, I recommend time durations of 10 to 25 minutes with five to 10 minutes rest in between. The total distance for this type of training should never total more than the race distance one is training for. The pulse rate after each tempo period should reach approximately five beats per minute less than maximum pulse. One should feel rested again before another tempo period is repeated.

Oxygen debt training is very important to accustom a racer to recover from the type of oxygen debt cross-country skiers run into in the early stages of a race and on uphills. This type of training involves going at maximum speed with a pulse rate very near maximum beats per minute. You should definitely feel a painful stiffening up of the legs during the later stages of each "oxygen debt" interval effort. Normally, I recommend speed periods of one to two minutes with five to six minutes of rest or jogging in between.

Sharon Firth, who, along with her sister Shirley, is one of the stars of the Canadian Nordic Ski Team. (Jarl Omholt-Jensen)

Again, this type of training has extreme effects on the body. Due to the importance of training *specifically* for a particular body movement or activity, I only recommend this type of training for the later climbing states of training on skis.

WEIGHT TRAINING

I understand that the US national nordic program has stirred some controversies with its heavy emphasis on weight training. In the early '70s Canada went through stages of experimental weight training, too. Along with most other nations, we have found weight training to be unsuccessful.

We have found that the stars of international cross-country racing are no stronger than the average person except in the specific double-poling and diagonal skiing movements. For a cross-country skier, it seems important to improve the oxygen transport system to the specific muscles used in skiing. If you enlarge many muscles, this will require more oxygen when you ski. If you train the wrong muscles, and this is easy to do with weights, then the oxygen transport system to these muscles will reduce and/or block the oxygen transport to the muscles you use when skiing.

I would only recommend weight training to those athletes who are below average in strength. And even here I would add the stipulation : the athlete must be absolutely sure that the weight training is as specific as possible to the body movements of skiing.

For others I will recommend they get their power training for the legs by doing eight to 10-second sprints on a steep uphill, and for the back and arms by roller skiing.

ROLLER SKIING

Since the East German breakthrough in the world championships at Vysoke Tatry, Czechoslovakia, in 1970, the training of arms for nordic skiers has received additional emphasis. The tremendous improvement in double poling the Germans demonstrated in Czechoslovakia can be attributed to their development and use of roller skis in training.

Today most of the top cross-country racers in the world spend about 20 to 50 percent of their dry-land training time on roller skis. I feel that the specific arm and back movement in roller skiing is so close to actual skiing that it is without a doubt the best upper body training for skiers.

It is obvious that the faster you ski the more important your arms become. In the diagonal technique on the flat, a slow skier may derive only 15 percent of his forward momentum from the arms, but an international champion gets as much as 25 to 30 percent of his momentum from the arms. He has to—if he is to ski as fast as possible.

If roller skis are not available or if there is no place to roller ski in your area, then I would recommend the use of an Exer-genie or Idar training apparatus. A varied program of stamina and interval (repetition) training on these devices is excellent and specific training for cross-country skiers.

HINTS ON TRAINING

I strongly recommend that every cross-country racer keep a training diary. By studying his past training diaries, the racer can figure out the percentages of the different types of training he has done. The most successful training ratios of interval, tempo, distance, roller skiing, running, skiing and strength training are very individualistic from racer to racer. In order for you to have an effective training program, you must find the most successful percentage ratio of the different types of training for your body type. Also remember to save your deep-down energy reserves for the important races. Do not drain these reserves in training.

Your training diaries will also enable you to find the best way to peak for races. Usually a sharp increase in anaerobic training with long rests in between training sessions will drastically raise your racing curve.

Finally, remember to keep a positive attitude, shut the negative things out— be a winner.

I believe we in Canada have arrived at the best way of training for the stage we are at now. However, I realize the Swedes train different in many ways, the East Germans train different again and so forth. The Norwegians have without a doubt had the most success with the smallest amounts of training. This might be a sign that they are using the most effective methods. But I think that besides finding the right formula between intensity and duration, the key to a successful program is that you believe 100 percent in the program you are following. Many racers try too many different methods and only become confused.

HOW TO DEVELOP GOOD TECHNIQUE

In this article I have chosen to discuss the fundamentals of the diagonal technique only. The topic of nordic skiing technique, however, does fascinate me and I do hope in the near future to write a book on it.

My approach to technique instruction differs somewhat from the conventional approach. Perhaps it's because I seldom deal with pupils at the beginner stage nowadays. But instead of teaching technique by the conventional method, I analyze the pupil's technique, explain his problem, what is causing the problem, and how to correct it. The corrective solution is seldom the same with two skiers, as their problem is usually caused by different faults.

In studying the skiing technique of North American skiers during the last 15 years, I'd say that our number one problem is weight shift. Many skiers drop their back ski, which causes a drag on their gliding ski. Others simply step forward instead of thrusting forcefully into the glide. I correct these mistakes by teaching a smooth and effective weight transfer.

The second most important thing I stress is what the Norwegians call "the kick." I call it the "push-off," as I feel the word "kick" is very misleading and often makes people literally *kick* backwards.

I teach the push-off by stressing complete weight transfer (this allows the snow crystals to bite into the wax for grip): the foot becomes stationary and pushes against the snow; the body moves forward; all your power should be exerted down and progressively back against the snow; the follow-through is important but no strength should be used after you have pushed off; the knee should become straight and then relaxed.

Furthermore, I teach blocked hips and shoulders, and straight and natural arm motions.

7
U.S.
Program

by Marty Hall
Head Coach, US Ski Team

If one thing stands out as unique, or close to it, in the US Ski Team training approach, it's the emphasis placed on weight training. "I think we're one of the few national teams to use weight training extensively," says head coach Marty Hall. This chapter consists of two articles by coach Hall. The first article is essentially his training guide for the US Cross-Country Ski Team. In the second, he describes (together with illustrations) the team's weight-training program.

Marty Hall, who is 37 (he was born in 1937), is from Hartford, Vermont. and is a graduate of the University of New Hampshire. A member of the '62 US Biathlon Team, he's been the US head nordic coach since 1972. Before that he coached the women's team. He has coached Martha Rockwell almost from the time she first started in the sport.

This training guide for the US Cross-Country Ski Team has evolved over the years from input from other national programs, the athletes, many coaches, our Sports Medicine Program and, of course, from me and the present coaching staff.

This guide is designed to give our skiers a general direction in their training. Through evaluation of their competitive records and from objective results in our Sports Medicine Testing Program, we are able to give specific direction to each athlete and assist that athlete in setting up his or her own individual training program.

SUGGESTED WEEKLY TIME ALLOTMENT SCHEDULE

Below is a suggested outline of what training objectives should be met each week, with appropriate changes for later months. These suggestions are given in terms of time as opposed to distance. The ranges given represent recommended time to be spent each week on the various forms of conditioning. Juniors and women can stay close to the lower limits, while serious senior men should aspire to the upper limits.

APRIL—rest and maintenance work.

MAY—10-16½ hours per week

    5-8½ hours—endurance
    1-1½ hours—ski-bounding with poles
    3-4 hours—strength training (three sessions)
    1-2½ hours—roller skiing

JUNE—10-16½ hours per week

    4-7 hours—endurance
    1-1½ hours—ski-bounding with poles
    3-4 hours—strength training (three sessions)
    1—1½ hours—interval and tempo training
    1-2 hours—roller skiing

JULY—12-18½ hours per week

    4-7 hours—endurance
    *1-1½ hours—ski-bounding with poles
    3-4 hours—strength training
    2-2½ hours—interval and tempo training
    2-3 hours—roller skiing
    *increase intensity over June.

AUGUST—12-18½ hours per week

    3-5 hours—endurance
    1-3 hours—ski-bounding with poles
    3-4 hours—strength training
    2-2½ hours—interval and tempo training
    3-4 hours—roller skiing.

SEPTEMBER—12-19½ hours per week

    3-4½ hours—endurance
    *2-3 hours—ski-bounding with poles
    3-4 hours—strength training
    2½-3½ hours—interval and tempo training
    3½-4½ hours—roller skiing
    *increase intensity over August.

OCTOBER—14½-20 hours per week

    3-4 hours—endurance
    *2-3 hours—ski-bounding with poles
    3-4 hours—strength training
    2½-4 hours—interval and tempo training
    4-5 hours—roller skiing (48-60 km/week)
    *increase intensity over September

NOVEMBER—14½-20 hours per week

    Same as October—but increase intensity.

Athletes should be on snow no later than November 15. Skiing should consist mainly of distance work, averaging 40-50 kilometers per day. The total distance skied by Christmas should be 1200-1500 kilometers. Also during this period, strength work should be done three times a week and some foot running up to two times per week. Intervals or tempo training on skis should not begin before the athlete has skied a total of 500 kilometers.

Workouts should range in time from 45 minutes to three hours.

Biking. Physiologists feel that when training on a bike, it takes about three miles of hard steady pedaling to equal one mile of foot running in ski type terrain.

PERSONAL (SECONDARY) TESTING

An athlete should be formally tested by his coach, or himself, about once a month to get a reading on how he is progressing in his conditioning. Below is a secondary testing procedure which is used periodically to check the progress of the US Ski Team athletes, and was used in the eastern US this summer for eastern athletes as well.

The important thing to remember about this testing procedure is that it is personal to each athlete, allowing him to plot his own progress against prior standards. This testing procedure is not so valid as to allow meaningful comparison of different athletes.

SECONDARY TESTING PROCEDURE

1. Bench press—maximum pressed in three tries. You must be able to press your own body weight or you are lacking in necessary upper body strength.

2. Sit-ups—maximum in one minute (on the flat with knees up, another person holding the feet). 55-60 repetitions in one minute.

3. Dips—maximum—no time limit. 15-25 or upper body strength and endurance are lacking.

4. Vertical jump—maximum height in three tries. 18 inches for women; 20 inches for men.

5. 15-minute run—on a level ¼-mile track. 2½ miles for women; 2¾ miles for men.

Test should be run in the above order.

SUGGESTED CROSS-COUNTRY TRAINING GUIDE

As a competitive sport, cross-country skiing places immense demands on the body's strength and endurance by utilizing almost all the body muscles in every movement. A good cross-country skier must have strength, endurance, coordination, speed and flexibility. The more all-round physical activities a skier can engage in during the off-season, the better he will be able to meet and overcome the demands of the sport.

The intent of this guide is not to outline a slavish training program for skiers to follow but to highlight those activities which are natural to a skier and will serve him best in his skiing. Within these activities we will note many of the methods and techniques of formal ski training, but certain knowledge of basic training techniques is assumed.

There are three principles, or better yet, "three secrets," of effective or good ski training—no matter how formal or informal that training may be. They are intensity, related movements, and strength.

Intensity—doing the physical activity in question at maximum effort. The only way to increase an athlete's maximum capacity for a work load is to push up his present maximum tolerance; thus, what is intense one month will not feel so intense the next month.

Related Movements—any movement or action that is directly related or similar to any of the skiing movements and is performed in dry-land training—e.g., roller skiing, ski-striding.

Strength—the development of the ability in an athlete to execute his actions with the power to make them effective, and to continually repeat the movement.

A skier should tailor his activities as much as possible to incorporate the above principles, thereby developing a fundamentally well-balanced program.

DRY-LAND ACTIVITIES

Below are a wide variety of dry-land training activities for skiers, along with suggestions on how they can modify these activities for the most effective development of physical fitness in cross-country skiing.

Incidentally, most skiers find support and encouragement as well as competitive objectives when they train as a group, and they also have more fun. All training, whether it's formal or informal, should be coordinated so that whenever possible there's a group present to do the day's training.

WARM-UP AND WARM-DOWN

This refers to the time before and after the workout spent in preparing the body by light running, exercises and stretching. An essential but most frequently neglected part of any workout schedule.

Warm-up—to get the muscles loosened, and increase circulation before substantial exertion. The warm-up should consist of jogging and light stimulating actions closely related to the movements to be undertaken in the workout.

Warm-down—to re-acclimate the body to an at-rest state from the demands of exertion. Done by light jogging, stretching and loosening exercises.

RUNNING

Running is the best single means to gain cardiovascular fitness but the necessary effects can be gained by many different methods. Some of the types of running workouts listed below can be done on a track, but all of these can be done on ski-type terrain. The more uphill running encountered the better, since strength, as well as endurance, is called into play. Certainly, as an athlete gets into the latter part of his pre-season conditioning program (i.e., fall) he should bring more uphill running into his workouts.

Types of running training:

1. *Tempo*—5 to 70 seconds. Repeated runs at near or maximum effort with extended rest. Pulse should be 100 beats per minute before repeating next sprint.

2. *Intervals*—50 seconds to 10 minutes. Repeated runs at a good pace with a short rest in between. Pulse should be 120 beats per minute before next run is started.

3. *Natural Intervals*—A longer, sustained run with periods of highly intense efforts, to be determined by the terrain. Pulse rate should go up to 180 beats per minute on the most intense efforts. Either pace or movement can be varied as follows for desired intensity:

> *Pace*—walk the downhills, run the flats and gradual up-
> hills and sprint the steep uphills;
> *Movement*—ski-walk the flats (fast!), ski-stride gradual
> uphills and ski-bound the steep uphills, walk the down-
> hills.

Natural interval workouts require a good selection of terrain and should be done for a specific time period rather than over a specific distance.

4. *Endurance*—A long, sustained run at a "steady state" level of effort. Anywhere from 6 to 15 miles. At the shorter end of the scale, the pace should be correspondingly faster. If you are not tired at the end of an endurance workout, don't go longer next time, go faster.

SKI-STRIDE SIMULATION

These are related ski movements to be utilized in hiking and running to develop leg strength and power.

1. *Ski-stride (ski-walk)*—A brisk striding forward, hips are dropped, and the forward moving leg goes strongly by the push-off leg, which is fully extended behind. The body is carried in a relaxed supple position, a bit forward, and the arms swing naturally; particularly effective on gradual uphills.

2. *Ski-bounding*—Comparable to ski-striding but done on a steeper hill with more vigor. Hips are low with a springing movement from one leg to the other, landing on a slightly bent front leg, with a fully extended back leg. Arm swing is coordinated to leg action.

SKI-BOUNDING WITH POLES

3. *Ski-bounding with poles*—Same movement as described in No. 2 above, except that poles are also used. Develops upper body strength and skiing coordination. Can be done as a full workout by repeating 35-75 second efforts, with full attention to technique. A few shorter (10-20 second) sprints can also be done, with no regard given to technique in these efforts. Ski-bounding can be done as repeated runs up the same slope, or, if a long slope is available, horizontal walks across the slope can be used for recovery before continuing to bound up the slope.

4. *"Hesitation" ski-bounding with poles*—each time you land on the front foot (ball of the foot) in the ski-bounding motion, hesitate so that the next move-

ment involves a definite and distinct thrust with opposite leg and pole. Hesitation should be long enough to ensure that no momentum from the previous step carries over.

5. *Indian dance (skipping)*—bound up a hill without poles in a vigorous skipping motion—opposite hand to leg, both coming up strongly as opposed to ahead.

The last three ski-simulation activities can be combined to make a single all-inclusive work-out. In all the above, close attention should be given to the technique as there is a close correlation between these exercises and actual skiing. Also, in ski-bounding, no hill should be used that is going to be steeper than any encountered during a cross-country ski race.

ROLLER–SKIING

Roller-skiing is the newest innovation to cross-country ski training. This practice is widely used in Europe since it does incorporate specific technique training with dry-land cardiovascular conditioning.

The same types of workouts used in running can be applied to roller skiing, except endurance distances can be longer than specified for running, up to 50 kilometers for senior men. Look elsewhere in this book for articles dealing specifically with roller skiing.

STRENGTH TRAINING

Through testing in our Sports Medicine Program, it has become apparent that the two areas American skiers are low in are upper body strength and leg power. The latter can be helped by incorporating a lot of uphill training into the running workouts. Strength training is not a factor in everyday living for most athletes, so it needs to be a very disciplined and demanding part of an athlete's training. To maintain your present strength, you need to lift weights two days a week and to gain strength requires three days of lifting a week.

Although lifting weights is the most common way to train for strength, it is not the only way to accomplish the objective. Natural strength training is possible in the form of, for example, pull-ups, dips, and extensive uphill running, all with a weighted pack or sand bag.

With any type of strength training, a good warm-up and thorough warm-down, both including stretching, is essential to maximum muscular development with adequate flexibility.

Armbands, Exer-genie, and Wall-Pulley Weights—methods highly used for the development of upper body strength through the simulation of the poling action.

Armbands can be made out of inner tubes, surgical tubing, shock cords, springs, and attached to any stationary object (tree, pole, wall) at about eye level. With one end in each hand, pull in an alternating fashion to simulate single poling, or pull both to simulate the double-poling action. Remember to stay flexed in the knees and hips.

The Exer-genie is now the most accepted method for pole simulation and upper body development. It can also serve as a complete weight program exerciser.

Cycling is excellent dry-land training for the development of leg strength and overall endurance. Shown here are US racers Martha Rockwell and Bob Gray. (US Ski Association photo)

OTHER MORE INFORMAL ACTIVITIES

These activities are more informal and general, but lend themselves to easy modification or adjustments so that specific training objectives can be realized.

Hiking—very good for leg and lower back strength and overall endurance. Adjustments: (1) pace—variable, faster (intensity); (2) Pack—additional weights (strength); (3) Movement—long, low stride with long arm movements (related movement); (4) Poles or hand weights—upper body development (strength).

Biking—excellent development of leg strength and overall endurance, especially the heart and lungs. Adjustments: (1) Pace—variable, fast, or maintained; (2) Duration—longer-slower, shorter-faster; (3) Terrain—hilly, flat or variable; (4) Racing—time trials, handicap races, sprints or pack races.

Swimming—very good for arm and leg strength and heart-lung development. Good factor of endurance can be developed. Adjustments: (1) Pace—variable, fast or maintained; (2) Duration—longer-slower, shorter-faster; (3) Diving—acrobatics and precision (coordination and agility); (4) Water games—water polo, racing.

Rowing, Kayaking and Canoeing—excellent upper body development, heart-lung development and builder of endurance. Adjustments: (1) Pace—fast, variable and maintained. (2) Duration—longer-slower, shorter-faster. Note: Kayaking and canoeing take precedence over rowing as the arm movement is a related movement to the poling action.

WEIGHT TRAINING
by Marty Hall

As mentioned earlier, through testing in our Sports Medicine Program, it has become very apparent that the two areas American skiers are low in are upper body strength and leg power. This program is designed to help you improve in these areas, and others.

Here are some of the ways in which you'll benefit by incorporating weight training into your regular training program.

1. You'll increase your strength.

2. You'll decrease the possibility of injury in your overall training.

3. As a result of added strength, you'll have greater explosive power and speed of movement.

4. Strength improves muscle endurance, that ability for the muscle to contract with power time after time, a factor so important in cross-country skiing.

5. The athlete who knows he is stronger has a psychological advantage over his opponent.

6. Strength training requires self-discipline, also another important factor in cross-country skiing.

There are two methods of weight training—weight-training for strength and weight training for endurance. We're not going to favor either of these. Instead, we're going to try to "split the difference" and accomplish both in this program.

Some pointers concerning correct technique in lifting:

1. Make sure you have performed some light exercise and jogging as a warm-up.

2. Full range of movement in an exercise is always necessary.

3. Always work in a safe situation—include a spotter if necessary.

4. When moving or lifting weights, always use the legs to start the lift--
    never the back.

5. Breathing correctly in lifting is important. Inhale when you're set to
    make the repetition and exhale as you complete it.

6. Between lifts, be sure to rest.

This program will require three sets of 10 repetitions for each lift. We will
use a progressive method in which 10 pounds are added between each set, for
example:

Bench Press	1st set	90 lbs.
	2nd set	100 lbs.
	3rd set	110 lbs.

When you can achieve 10 repetitions with the required weight in the third
set, increase the weight for the first set by 10 pounds the next time you lift.

This program requires you to lift three days a week with a rest day between.
Your schedule could be Monday, Wednesday and Friday, for example, or Tuesday,
Thursday and Saturday.

1. Bench Press
For the chest, triceps, and deltoids. Done in a supine position. First set
can be half the body weight.

2. Stiff Legged Dead Lift
Stand with feet in front of a barbell, shoulder-width apart and toes pointed
straight ahead. Bend down, keeping legs straight, and grasp bar with hands
shoulder-width apart, palms facing backward. Keeping legs straight, come to
fully erect position. Lower weight to floor and repeat for prescribed number of
repetitions. Perform exercise while standing with feet on six-inch raised platform
and barbell on floor. (You may have to start on a two- or three-inch platform at
first.) Start with half the body weight for first set.

3. Bent Rowing
Starting position: Toes near the bar, feet shoulder-width apart, knees straight,
back straight, hips flexed, hands gripping bar shoulder-width apart, palms facing
backward. Lift bar to lower chest area by bending elbows and pulling the arms
upward. Pull bar to lower chest area, then lower to starting position. Repeat
for prescribed number of repetitions. Use one half to two-thirds body weight
for first set.

4. Squats
A barbell is held in a position in front of the chest with palms facing forward,
feet twelve inches apart. Squat down to a 90-degree bend, keeping the back
straight. Return to the starting position. Let heels raise off floor as you squat
down. Use half body weight for first set.

5. Pullover
Light weights—supine position. Grasp barbell at shoulder width behind head.
Girls should be careful on this lift. Use floor rather than bench.

6. Sit-ups

On inclined plane—three sets of 25 repetitions; when you can do this put a five-pound weight behind the neck. Start from supine position on plane, ankles firmly held, arms behind head. Curl up to a semi-sitting position at the same time flexing the knees. Alternate sit-up sets with back extension exercise.

7. Back extension

Do three sets of 25 repetitions—use weights. Lie in prone position, face down over end of table. End of table should hit body at groin level. Partner or belt holds legs down against table. Start with chin close to floor, hands behind head, raise head and upper body in a back-arching movement as high as possible. Return to position with nose close to floor. Repeat for prescribed number of repetitions.

8. Front Leaning Wall Squats

Position feet two feet from wall, shoulder-width apart. Lean forward, placing hands on wall at shoulder height. Bend elbows and lean forward until head is three inches from wall. Keeping hands stationary on wall and head three inches from wall, flex knee and squat until the angle of knee bend is 90 degrees, then straighten leg and return to starting position. Always keep head three inches from wall. Do four sets of 20 repetitions alternating legs. Use knapsack with weights or rocks for increased resistance.

9. Press

For the shoulders and triceps. Hold barbell at shoulder-width hand spacing. Stand with legs apart; press weights rapidly up and slowly back down. Use one third body weight for first set.

10. Toe Raisers

Feet flat on floor, hold bar in front of shoulders with hands. Raise upon toes, lifting weights. Do four sets of 20 repetitions using 100 pounds to start.

An important facet of your weight-training program should be the recording of your lifting and the progress you make. This will also help you in becoming more disciplined and regular in your lifting.

8

The Racers

SIXTEN JERNBERG

The Swede, Sixten Jernberg, born in western Dalarna's backwoods country February 6, 1929, is the foremost cross-country skier of all time. Between 1954 and 1964 he won four Olympic gold medals, three silver medals, and two bronze medals. He became world champion four times and won two world championship bronze medals. In addition, he won 15 individual Swedish championships and five gold medals in the relay. Of course, Sixten also won a series of other international competitions, including two Vasaloppet victories.

He became a folk hero and legend even during his active career. This extremely strong boy from Dalarna with the wild competitive spirit lives on in Swedish hearts. In a TV poll in Sweden this year, 10 years after he stopped competing, Sixten was chosen by a large margin as Sweden's best athlete of all time. And he had to contend with heroes such as Gert Fredriksson (canoeist with six Olympic gold medals, one Olympic silver and one Olympic bronze, together with four world championships, 14 Scandinavian championships and 71 Swedish championships), Gunder Hagg (a middle distance runner who broke 15 world records during his career), professional soccer idols such as Gunnar Gren and Nacka Skoglund, the cyclist Gösta Fåglum Pettersson and many others.

What was it that made Sixten Jernberg the great cross-country skier he was? How did he train? The answer is very simple: he worked hard physically on his job, he trained hard, and he had a rebellious temperament and a will far beyond the ordinary. He was the ideal competitor who never acknowledged defeat.

BEGAN SKIING WHEN HE LEARNED TO WALK

Sixten grew up in Lima, a little village in the great forests of western Dalarna (not too many miles from the starting point of the Vasaloppet in Salen, near the Norwegian border). The area always has plenty of snow, and Sixten began to ski at the same time he learned how to walk. Right after finishing school he began to work in the forest, and here he laid the foundation for his enormous physical strength. His first major international appearance came at the world championships at Falun in 1954 where he finished fourth in the 30-kilometer, seventh in the 15-kilometer, and 12th in the 50-kilometer. Moreover, Sixten skied on the Swedish team which took home the bronze medal in the men's 4 x 10-km relay. At the Olympic Games in 1956 he won his first gold medal in major international competition, and thereafter he won at least one gold medal at every world championship and Olympic competition up to and including 1964.

The key to Sixten's great strength was his woodcutting job in the forest.

"That was different from today's oft spoiled stars who sit on the sofa between training sessions," says Sixten with a gleam in his eye. "In some ways it was more honest before. Then you didn't get things without working hard to make your way in the world. Today a guy doesn't have to work; between training sessions he takes it easy and is happy, and he gets money from training allowances and stipends."

Sixten worked hard during the summer months in order to be able to ski full time during the winter. He cut wood from morning until evening.

"I was often so tired that I wasn't able to straighten out my back when I was supposed to eat the sandwiches and coffee I had with me. I had to sit doubled up and eat the food.

"When evening came it was time for training. In heavy working boots and overalls it was off right through the forest, up the mountain sides (high hills) and then back to the forest cabin which I lived in when I was out on forest work.

"A dip in the ice cold mountain lake and then a little food before it was time to hit the sack. When the sun came up it was time to begin chopping wood again, and when evening came a new training session was waiting. Those were difficult times, but as I said it was a matter of earning enough money so that I was able to get by during the winter. Your body was always tired, and the training session didn't last longer than 50 minutes. But that was after a whole day's hard work and in heavy forest clothing."

At the beginning of autumn there were longer tours for Sixten. Now he let up a bit on the work in the forest and devoted more time to training or long hunting tours in the wilderness terrain.

"Sometimes I stuffed as much food as I could into myself in the morning and took off on a long tour of four to five hours. In the fall, I would run mile after mile over hard terrain; sometimes the devil possessed me, and if I came to a lake which wasn't overly wide, I swam across it instead of running around it. Then it took up to a half hour before you thawed out enough so that the pace became comfortable again. But I always thought that I would be thankful for this extra effort of the will when the time for competition came and the conditions were bad."

NO GIMMICKS, JUST HARD WORK

It might be interesting to look at Sixten's training book from this period. Here was his training during mid-November one year:

Nov. 7 — 1 hour's running in the forest (hard cross-country)

Nov. 8 — 5 hours running and walking

Nov. 9 — 1½ hours running in forest

Nov. 10 — 2½ hours running

Nov. 11 — no training. 7½ hours cutting wood

Nov. 12 — 1½ hours running in forest

Nov. 13 — 1½ hours running

Nov. 14 — 3 hours running

Nov. 15 — 3½ hours forest and road running

Nov. 16 — 1 hour hard running over very difficult terrain (ran up a mountain side until he came to snow line)

Nov. 17 — Began to ski

The week between November 8th and 14th above consisted of 15 hours hard training plus a good seven hours of hard forest work. Thus, there was never a question of any gimmicks in Sixten Jernberg's training. It was simply a question of hard work and hard training. That gave him the physical and psychological strength which made him the great competitor he was—and still is today!

As recently as January, 1974, a good young Swedish racer in his 20's got the surprise of his life during a competition in Sixten's hometown Lima (Sixten still lives there. Today he has a popular resort on his old training grounds.) The skier came up behind someone he thought was a middle-aged spectator in the way on the track. There were difficult skiing conditions on the hard slopes, but no matter what the skier did he could not catch up with the older skier in front. Approaching the finish the skier recognized the older man. It was none other than Sixten, who had taken a swing on the track to see how the course was.

After his retirement, Sixten got a job as a representative for a ski manufacturer, but he never lost contact with the hard forest labor.

"It gave natural strength, and then you didn't have to sit around and lift weights some place or pull rubber hoses."

Sixten has always been an energetic person, and when he finished as an active skier, he devoted his strength and energy to clearing an area in the forest by himself and building his resort—fifteen cottages, a swimming pool, training track, golf course, and fish ponds.

HIS OWN MAN

Unique as a competitor, Sixten Jernberg is equally unique as a person. And this is what has kept the Swedish ski federation thus far from exploiting the enormous experience Sixten has as a skier. He has always gone his own way. He has expressed his thoughts even if they didn't always please the leaders. This is clear from, among other things, what Sixten tells about the training camps he participated in during his active career.

"If they said we should run left, then I ran right."

If he was out with the others sometime on a long tour, he would often shout "full speed home" when there were a few kilometers left to camp just for the pleasure of seeing the others chase after him as hard as they could. Sixten enjoyed that.

He was always full of mischief and still is today, but this was a champion of the purest water and an unusually considerate person.

It is now 10 years since Sixten retired, but as the earlier anecdote indicates, he is still in very good condition. It takes a lot of training for a younger skier to be able to hang with Sixten on a tour through the forest.

Earlier we offered a sample of Sixten's running training. Let's conclude by looking briefly at his actual ski training. It was just as uncomplicated as his running training—he got on the skis and skied, up one hill and down another, preferably over as difficult a terrain as possible. Two to three hours a day was the normal ration, but at times it was six, seven, or eight hours of skiing in light snow. This was when he went out on hunting tours.

Summing up his views on training, Sixten asserts that the only approach for a serious skier is year-round training. He said that back when he was a racer and he still says it today. You have to keep active even during the period when there are no ski competitions. You maintain your conditioning in the spring, and then you add to it a little, day by day, until it's time for putting on the skis again and setting off on the best thing of all—skiing.

Remember also, says Sixten, that from first to last it is you yourself that athletic success depends on. Be thankful for the help you can get, but if possible never depend on it.

—Lennart Strand

THOMAS MAGNUSSON

Presently one of the superstars of nordic skiing. 24 years old. Lives in Delsbo, Sweden. Won a gold medal in the 30 kilometers and a bronze medal in the 50 kilometers at the '74 nordic championships. Top-ranked skier in the world in '73 and a winner of numerous international races. Has twice accomplished what only legendary Swedish skiers Sixten Jernberg, Mora-Nisse Karlson and Assar Ronnlund managed to do before him—win all three races (15, 30 and 50 kilometers) at the Swedish championships during the same week.

Born July 2, 1950 at Motala, Sweden. 6'0½", 174 lbs. Started competing seriously in 1967 at age 17. Occupation: public relations man.

Likes all distances, all snow conditions, all types of courses. Coached by David (Dalle) Johansson, former Vasaloppet winner.

Training: Thomas Magnusson is one of the hardest training nordic skiers of all time. During the winter, for example, he averages 40 hours a week on skis! As his teammates on the Swedish "A" team say of him: "Thomas is number one, and it's okay, because when you train as hard as he does you deserve to be number one."

April is Magnusson's lone easy month during the year. In May it's back to serious training. From May until the snow arrives, he trains 20 hours per week.

Fifty percent of his training is hard foot running (he increased the quality of his running training after the '74 world championships at Falun, Sweden) and the other 50% is on roller skis ("The latter gives me the strength training that I need.") He does very little straight interval training. But most of his running is over hilly woodland or through reindeer moss and bogs, and can rightly be called natural interval training.

Magnusson starts skiing in November—five to six hours daily at a steady pace (which is so fast that a normally trained athlete can stay with him for no more than a few kilometers). During the race season he cuts back a little on the distance but increases the pace. For the bulk of the winter, however, he skis up to 40 hours per week, most of it at a fast, steady pace.

As a skier, Magnusson has practically everything. He is technically perfect, extremely strong and can handle all types of courses and snow conditions. In addition, he has tremendous competitive spirit and a willingness to train far harder than the norm.

"Yes, almost too much," says coach Johansson, "The problem with Thomas is not getting him to train, but rather getting him not to train too much. As far as Thomas' determination to win, during the 25 years I have been involved with cross-country skiing I have met only one person who can compare with Thomas as to tenacity, psyche and temperament, and that is Sixten Jernberg."

Magnusson is such a dedicated athlete that in 1972, when Sweden had a snow shortage, he laid out a narrow snow path about 1000 yards long and skied back and forth on this strip up to 60 kilometers a day. In October of the same year he found snow on a mountain road up in the wilderness and he skied a nine-kilometer stretch back and forth all day long for several weeks in succession.

Magnusson was interviewed by Lennart Strand in the May '74 issue of *Nordic World*. The following questions and answers are excerpted from that interview.

How do you relax?

I almost never relax, no time for it. I train, work, eat and rest, and train again. The hours left over—if any—I devote to other sports, like watching soccer.

You're known for training tremendously hard. How do you set up your program?

I don't have any day-by-day program. Rather I set up a plan to ski so-and-so many hours in such-and-such a month. Certainly I train a lot, but I have built myself up to it during the past few years—and only recently has it become so many hours.

How do you manage this heavy training you do?—up to 40 hours a week in winter. Don't you now and then think that you train too hard? Will you continue in the same fashion?

As I said, I've built myself up to it over the years, and now I feel I can take the training I'm doing. I plan to train just as many hours the coming year. I won't increase the quantity, but I will increase the quality. Thus, I figure on training just as many hours in 1974 as I did in 1973, and in addition I will perhaps improve the quality in certain sessions. I don't think it'll be too hard; on the contrary, I think I'll be able to take it.

JUHA MIETO

Like Magnusson, Mieto is one of the superstars of nordic skiing. The massive 25-year-old Finn (he's 6'5¼", 220 lbs.) won the silver medal behind Magnusson in the 30 kilometers at the '74 world championships, and he was fourth in the 30 kilometers at the '72 Winter Olympics in Sapporo. Among his many international victories are three wins in the last two years ('74 and '73) at the world famous Holmenkollen in Oslo. Mieto (pronounced *Me-a-toe*) is considered to be the world master at waxing for wet snow conditions.

Born November 20, 1949 in Kurikka, Finland where he still lives. He started competing in '67 at age 16. Self-coached. Occupation: sports instructor.

His favorite distance is 30 kilometers. He prefers wet snow (naturally) and a varying course with a good track.

Training: He starts his training program for the ski season May 1. In the beginning he does one workout per day. For example:

Monday –	walking over mossy terrain	2 hours
Tuesday –	roller skiing	25 km
Wednesday –	running	20 km
Thursday –	rowing	2 hours
Friday –	walking-running	20 km
Saturday –	roller skiing	20 km
Sunday –	orienteering	12 km

Towards the end of the summer he does two workouts per day.

Mieto's ski training begins in November. For two months he skis about 50 kilometers per day, "slowly and tranquilly." He completes his build-up for the competitive season with two weeks of hard quality training at the beginning of January. During this two-week period, he skis 10 kilometers as fast as he can in the morning and 4 x 2 kilometers as fast as he can in the afternoon.

Mieto offers these additional comments on training: "Every skier should really know himself and know what kind of training system suits him. Training must be individual."

SVEN-AKE LUNDBACK

Twenty-seven years old. Lives in Lulea, Sweden. Gold medalist in the 15-kilometer at the '72 Winter Olympics in Sapporo, Japan. Finished fourth in the

50-kilometer at the '74 world championships. Winner of many international races.

Born Jan. 26, 1948 in Siknas, Sweden. 5'9¼", 146 lbs. Started competing when he was 17. Self-coached. Formerly an electrician, now a public relations man.

Favorite distance is 15 kilometers. Prefers hard tracks in wintry weather and hilly courses.

Training: *Summer*—200-250 kilometers per week (running and roller skiing). He runs at a steady to hard pace for approximately two hours each day. Plus, he roller skis three times a week.

Winter—350-400 kilometers of skiing per week. He does four to five hours of skiing every day in the early season. Later in the season, he skis three to four hours per day at a harder pace. He increases the quality still more just before and during the competitive season.

Lundback doesn't do as much quantity as most other top class skiers in Sweden and other European countries, but he is known for having an intense program. Most of his training consists of quality workouts.

BOB GRAY

Thirty-five years old, from Putney, Vermont. US 50-kilometer champion in '71 and '72, and 15-kilometer champion in '61. Placed 27th in 1970 Vasaloppet. Member of the '62, '66, '70 and '74 US FIS teams, and the '68 and '72 Winter Olympic teams.

Born April 25, 1939, in Putney, Vermont. 5'11", 165 lbs. Started competing in 1953, at age 14. Coached by John Caldwell, Bob Beattie, Tauno Pulkinen, Al Merrill and Marty Hall. Independent business man.

Favorite distance: 50 kilometers. Likes klister conditions, a hard track and a hilly course with few flats.

Training: Never trained year-round until 1969 ("I was never able to train as much as I should have because of job and family obligations"). His best year of skiing was 1970 which also was his best year of training. That year's training is described below:

April-May—(15 hours training per week) Easy running in the woods. Long hike-run on Sundays with 20-pound pack.

May-July—(15-20 hours per week) Easy running, hill climbs with poles, Sunday hikes with pack, biking.

August-September—(20 hours per week) Morning runs (six miles), hill climbs with poles, Sunday hikes (10-20 miles) with packs, long trail hike (270 miles in 10 days), biking, interval runs.

September-November—(20 hours per week, two workouts per day) Hill climbs with poles, hill climbs with pack (20 pounds), cross-country running, roller skiing, Sunday hike-run (15-20 miles).

November-December—(20 hours per week) Skiing two hours per day ("In November we got on snow in Winter Park, Colorado, for 10-15 days and did 300 kilometers of concentrated skiing"), dry-land hill climbs with pack, three times a week.

December-March—Racing two-three times per week (average total distance: 30 kilometers), ski training two-three hours a day (except when racing totalled 50-60 kilometers per week), dry-land hill climbs with pack or running two times per week.

Comments: "Once the ski racing season started I always tried to include an *easy* morning run (especially when travelling) to include light calisthentics and stretching exercises. It is very difficult once the ski season starts to retain your fall cardiovascular conditioning because skiing is basically much easier mile per mile, hour per hour, than running. So I also tried to get in a *hard uphill* foot run a couple of time per week plus basic strength work such as push-ups and sit-ups."

BILL KOCH

Top-ranked male nordic racer in the US in '73-'74 season at age 19. Considered one of the best prospects US has of winning internationally. Became first American to win a medal in international championship cross-country competition when he finished third at the European Junior Championships in Autrans, France, in '74. Other '74 accomplishments included: second in the Holmenkollen Junior; third in the 15-kilometer at the North American Championships (only six seconds behind Walter Demel of West Germany and four seconds behind world champion Thomas Magnusson); and first overall in the US Ski Team's Samsonite Nordic Series.

Born in Brattleboro, Vermont, June 7, 1955. Lives in Guilford, Vt. 5'10", 155 lbs. Began alpine skiing at age three, ski jumping at age six. At age eight, he started cross-country skiing so he could compete in the nordic combined. Qualified for the US Nordic Combined "B" Team at age 15. In 1970 he won the nordic combined in the Swiss Junior Championships. Switched to cross-country skiing exclusively in '72 after a knee injury on one of his jumps at the US Olympic Trials. Coached by Marty Hall. Full-time nordic racer.

Due to his age, still races short distances only. But favors courses which are very demanding—lots of vertical, steep winding downhills with sharp corners.

Training: *Spring* (April, May, June)—"During this time my main purpose in training is to have fun. After the long competitive season, I try to get back some general strength to have a broader "base" from which I can go a step higher than the year before with my specific cross-country strength work during the summer and fall. I do some training every day but high intensity work like hill running only two-three times a week. Otherwise, I ride a bicycle, hike, alpine ski on Mt. Washington, rock climb, roller ski, go on speed-hike exploring excursions, clear trails, cut wood..."

Summer (July-August)—"I spent last summer ('74) in Switzerland at high altitude—skiing cross-country, distance hiking with a pack and mountaineering. I tried to do as much vertical as possible in any form—hiking, skiing, running or climbing. I think it's a good idea to keep in touch with your sport by doing some low-key "fun" skiing in training. I become very stimulated by mountains."

Fall (September, October)—"This fall I spent all my time roller skiing, distance running, hill running and working with an Exer-genie. I did each of the first three a *minimum* of twice a week and tried to pull Exer-genie every day. Once a week I did a distance roller-ski tour of about 50 kilometers. The other times I'd roller ski up long hills of 10-15 miles. I also worked in some roller-ski uphill intervals of about two minutes."

Koch (the name is pronounced *coke*) experienced an impressive performance jump from '73 to '74 because of a large increase in his training. He biked over 2000 kilometers, roller skied close to 700 kilometers, ran a great deal and skied over 2000 kilometers prior to the world and European championships.

Additional comments: "One of the most important things about training is that you've got to enjoy it. You should have your training so set up that each day you look forward to the next. Each workout you do should be done with some purpose. You should know *why* you are doing what you're doing. Don't just go out and follow someone else's schedule just because it's the way that person trains. On the other hand, be open to *all* new ideas until you've proven to yourself that they aren't for you. If you operate with this type of individuality, you will build up self-respect, confidence and pride, which are so important to becoming a top-notch racer."

ERNIE LENNIE

Twenty-one years old, lives near the Arctic Circle in Fort Norman, Northwest Territories, Canada. Canadian 30-kilometer champion in '74 and Canadian junior champion in the 10 kilometers in '70.

Born December 20, 1953, in Aklavik, Northwest Territories. 5'8", 141 lbs. Started competing when he was 12. Coached by Bjorger Pettersen. Student.

Likes all distances but seems to do best at the longer ones (particularly 30 kilometers). Favors cold snow and varied terrain.

Training: May and June are his easiest months; he does some ski touring (Fort Norman still has snow at this time of year) and easy running. In July, he begins serious training, running approximately five hours per week in the woods. In August and September he does a lot of running—310 kilometers per month, mostly steady distance runs. October is his hardest training month (66 hours). In addition to approximately 550 kilometers of running, he does roller skiing and weight training. In November and early December he skis as much as possible (30-60 kilometers per day) to "gear up" for the racing season.

CHARLES BANKS

Age 51, from Duluth. Has won several US Ski Association central division championships. He was the '74 50-and-over champion in Minnesota's Telemark Birkebeiner, skiing 50 kilometers in 3:28:55. He was a high school nordic skiing champion in 1942.

Born November 21, 1923, in Duluth, Minnesota. 5'9", 160 lbs. Self-coached now, previously coached by Pete Fosseide. He's a high school teacher and coach (Duluth Central High School).

Prefers the 30 kilometers, cold powder snow and hilly courses.

Training: Runs 5-10 kilometers (sometimes 15 kilometers) over hilly terrain with his dog three times per week. Says he's "too old" to train more seriously; he used to run farther in his younger days. In his running, he follows the nordic course he has laid out on his property north of Duluth.

He believes in more variety in training for his high school team (he coaches Duluth Central's nordic team). He says, "Varied year-round training is best—running, cycling, weight training, arm bands, hill running with poles, etc."

JOHN DAY

Age 66. Lives in Gold Hill, Oregon. Received considerable publicity when he took up the sport at age 52, announcing that his ambition was to make the '64 US Winter Olympic team! Never got to try out for the team but has compiled a fine record since then as a senior (over 40) skier. Winner of the 1973 Senior Olympics cross-country event, and third place finisher in the same competition in '74. Has been the first over-40 finisher in several Oregon nordic races. In '64 he was given the Norwegian Ski Association Special Award for being the first (and thus far only) skier to make four complete trips to the top of Hardanger Jokulen and back to Finse in one day (a total distance of 100 kilometers). Was awarded the Cross-Country Skier of the Decade Award (1960-1970) by the Oregon Nordic Club and the Pacific Northwest Ski Association. Also races bikes and is an experienced mountaineer.

Born August 20, 1909, in Aberdeen, Wash. 6'1", 165 lbs. Has been coached by John Woxen, Oslo, Norway; Dr. Nils Eie, Oslo; and Trigve Brohdal, Ringkollen, Norway. Rancher. Former chairman of ski touring for the US Ski Association, presently the US director for citizen skiing (cross-country) with the FIS.

His favorite distance is 50 kilometers. Likes courses with long climbs, long downhills, and few turns (since he has a permanently stiff ankle from a mountaineering accident).

Training: During the summer he races bicycles (he won a silver medal in cycling at the '74 Senior Olympics in Los Angeles).

Of his year-round training, he says, "I used to grind myself down seven days a week on a fairly exhaustive training program. Now, after reading all the literature I could find, I have backed off and follow a more casual approach.

"The Norwegian national team coach Kristen Kvello told me at the North American championships at Big Sky, Montana, last year ('74) that they use long, slow distance (about 75-80 percent effort) in their training program. He told me they dropped interval training like a hot rock after using it for a year with their team. Their skiers get interval training on every hill they ski up anyway.

"I now ski 15 kilometers three times a week in winter and 50 kilometers once a week. As a fill-in, I use an ergometer (a stationary exercise bicycle), an exercise treadmill and resistance-type weight training."

NORM OAKVIK

Age 51. One of the finest over-40 skiers in the US. Has been a nordic competitor for many years. He was first in the US nordic combined championships in '55, and first in the North American cross-country championships in '54.

Born February 23, 1923, in Minneapolis, Minn. 5'6", 135 lbs. Self-coached. Nordic ski distributor.

Likes any distance up to 30 kilometers, and hilly courses with tight turns. Likes the challenge of tricky snow conditions.

Training: His pre-season training from April through November includes weight training, ski-striding on the flat, ski-bounding with poles up steep hills, interval and fast distance running. His other summer activities are bicycling and tennis.

 ## HELENA TAKALO

One of the world's best female skiers. Twenty-seven years old, from Pyhakumpu, Finland. In the '72 Winter Olympics at Sapporo, Japan, she was second in the relay, fifth in the 10-kilometer and eighth in the five-kilometer. She finished third in the 10-kilometer at the '74 world championships at Falun, Sweden.

Born October 28, 1947, in Nivala, Finland. 5'1½", 123 lbs. Started competing in 1964 when she was 17. Coached by Immo Kuutsa, Finnish national coach.

Likes five and 10-kilometer distances, snow temperatures between -5 and -10 degrees C., and courses that are hilly and gently sloping.

Training: Begins immediately after competition finishes. The training in the spring is very light, but becomes harder by the autumn. Trains every day in the summer and twice a day in the fall. Summer training consists of walking or running, and she roller skis four times a week. Skiing begins in November and her competitive racing season lasts from December to April.

SHIRLEY FIRTH

Along with her identical twin sister, Sharon, one of the stars of the Canadian national team. Outstanding record in North American competition. In '69, '70 and '71 she swept the women's events at both the Canadian and North American championships, winning the five and 10 kilometers, and being on the winning 3x5-kilometer relay team. She's been the Canadian 10-kilometer champion the last two years ('73 and '74). In the North American championships, she won the five-kilometer in '73 and the 10-kilometer in '74 (with sister Sharon finishing second). Both girls live in Inuvik, Northwest Territories.

Born December 31, 1953, in Aklavik, Northwest Territories. 5'4½", 116 lb. Started competing in 1968, when 13 years old. Coached by Bjorger Pettersen. Student (part-time), skier (full-time).

Likes both the five and 10 kilometers, and all types of courses. Prefers cold snow conditions.

Training: *May* – Start of training. Distance running, also competing in any foot races available.

June – Distance running at least four times a week.

July – Roller skiing and distance running at least five-six times per week, also some sprints and hikes.

August – Distances and interval running seven times a week. Roller skiing seven times a week.

September – Mainly distance running (longer runs than before) and interval, tempo (oxygen debt) training.

October – Long distance, interval and tempo training. Roller skiing seven days per week.

November – Getting into skiing. Easy skiing at first, long distance skiing later. Continues running at least twice a week.

December-April – Racing.

SHARON FIRTH

Second to her sister in both the five and 10 kilometers and member of the winning relay teams at the '69 and '70 Canadian championships and the '70 and '71 North American championships. Third in the junior five-kilometer at the Swedish Ski Games at Falun, Sweden, in '70. First in the five-kilometer at the '71 US championships and first overall in the '72 Trans-Am Series. Second in the 10-kilometer at the '74 North American Championships.

Born December 31, 1953, in Aklavik, Northwest Territories. 5'4", 118 lbs. Started competing in '68, when 13 years old. Coached by Bjorger Pettersen. Student (part-time), skier (full-time).

GV
854.9
C 7
72 /24634
CAMROSE LUTHERAN COLLEGE
Library